Junior Showmanship

from
Hand to Lead

The Complete Handbook
for
Junior Handlers

Mary A. Miller

Alpine
Blue Ribbon Books

An Imprint of Alpine Publications

Junior Showmanship from Hand to Lead: The Complete
Handbook for Junior Handlers

Library of Congress Cataloging-in-Publication Data

Miller, Mary A., 1957–
    Junior showmanship from hand to lead: the complete handbook for
    junior handlers / Mary A. Miller.
      101p. 15.2 x 22.9cm.
      Includes bibliographical references and index.
      ISBN 0–931866–66–9
      1. Dog shows– Junior showmanship classes– Handbooks, manuals,
etc.– Juvenile literature.   [1. Dogs– Showing. 2. Dog shows.]
I. Title.
SF425. 13.M55 1994
636.7'0888–dc20   94–1099
                                                                  CIP
                                                                   AC

First Printing March, 1994.
1 2 3 4 5 6 7 8 9 0
Printed in the United States of America

Cover Photo by Kent Dannen
Text illustrations by David Blondell unless otherwise noted
Design and layout: Alpine Publications

Table of Contents

This book is dedicated to my first Dalmatian, FRITZ III, the dog that introduced me to the sport of dog showing; and to my mother and father, who taught me that with determination you can achieve your highest goals in life.

Introduction

Junior Showmanship is a competition offered at kennel club-sponsored dog shows or matches for boys and girls between the ages of 10 and 18. Its purpose is to introduce you, the dog fanciers of tomorrow, to the sport of dog showing, and to provide classes designed to help you develop and improve your dog-handling skills. Judging is based solely on your ability to present your dog properly. With very few exceptions, any purebred dog is eligible to compete. You do not need a dog of championship quality to compete.

Junior Handling, as it is sometimes referred to, has served many exhibitors as one of the ground floor educations to bigger achievements in the dog world, such as becoming a licensed judge, dog handler, or successful breeder. Junior Showmanship offers a variety of learning experiences. You will meet other young people with whom you can exchange thoughts and ideas. You could even be selected as the winner of the prestigious Westminster Junior Showmanship competition or the World Junior Handling competition.

Hard work is most definitely ahead of you! But with love and pride in your dog and confidence in yourself, you will no doubt be successful at Junior Handling. You may not have yet imagined what new doors this may open to you with dogs.

It was that confidence that sparked me into going to my first dog show with a dog in one hand and my Dad's fishing tackle box filled with grooming supplies in the other. When I left that day with my first blue ribbon at my first dog show, I knew that I would be dedicated to this sport forever. I read every book I could on dogs. Since I did not come from a family interested in dogs, my show dog was my pet. Reading books gave me a good base knowledge on how to show. And with that, I gained the confidence in myself to go into the ring and do the very best I could.

That is why I wrote this book — to help you learn and succeed in this sport as I did. There were many things I could not find in books, but learned from experience in showing. I have included some of these, so that maybe you won't be caught making the same mistakes.

After years of showing in Junior Handling, I decided to obtain my Junior Showmanship judge's license from the American Kennel Club. Today, after many years of judging Junior classes, I still get a great thrill when I see a Junior Handler and his dog working in brilliant teamwork.

I sincerely hope that this book will help you to achieve such teamwork, and also to add a new dimension to your life. I know that you will find Junior Showmanship competition exciting and educational, and perhaps most of all, very satisfying.

Mary A. Miller
December 1993

Acknowledgments

Thanks to Bell Fenton and Verna Parker, who helped encourage me when I was getting started, and to all the helpful hands that were always there to help me with my dogs through the years.

A special thank you to Sheila Wymore, who from the start inspired me to put all my thoughts and ideas on paper, so that I could now share with other Junior Handlers all my experiences.

Last, I would like to remember all the other Junior Handlers that I had the pleasure of meeting, and who were invariably there to share all the victories, as well as the defeats.

Judith Strom

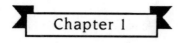

Chapter 1

What Is Junior Showmanship?

History

The idea of junior showmanship first came into existence over half a century ago when Leonard Brumby, Sr., created the Children's Handling Class to get children more involved in dog shows. Brumby saw many children being excluded from show-day activities, and consequently, many were bored and restless.

The first Children's Handling Class was held at the Westbury Kennel Club Show on Long Island, New York, in 1932. The classes were listed in the *premium list* (or show entry form) as follows:

> Class A: Boys under 14 years of age
> Class B: Girls under 14 years of age

After a successful first year, the Westbury Kennel Club held the Class again in 1933. This time the classes were divided further for boys and girls under 15 years of age and for those under 10 years of age. The only requirement was to bring a dog that could be controlled in the ring. Everyone who participated in the Class received candy.

Other kennel clubs that witnessed the success of the Class were quick to pick up the idea. In 1933, the Westminster Kennel Club held its first Children's Handling Championship. Anyone who had won a first place in a Children's Handling Class during the past year was eligible to compete for the Grand Challenge Trophy.

Through the years, there have been many changes in the class. In 1951, the name was officially changed to *Junior Showmanship* (sometimes called *Junior Handling*). Since then, classes have been divided into skill designations, such as Novice and Open, and further subdivided into age groups.

It wasn't until 1971 that Junior Showmanship received official American Kennel Club (AKC) recognition, and rules were established to guide Junior handlers and their judges in the ring. (For a copy of the current rule book, "Junior Showmanship Regulations, Judging Guidelines, and Guidelines for Juniors," write to the AKC Events Records Department, 51 Madison Avenue, New York City, NY 10010.)

Today, much of the idea of junior showmanship remains the same: to provide entertainment and education to youths between the ages of 10 and 18. Once a young person reaches his or her eighteenth birthday, he or she is no longer eligible to compete.

Much emphasis is still placed on qualifying for competition at the nation's premier dog show, Westminster. It now takes eight first-place wins to qualify for "the Garden."

The Basics 🐕

You don't need a dog of championship quality to participate in Junior Showmanship classes. In these classes, it is not the dog that is being judged, it is your ability to <u>handle</u> the dog.

The key to success in Junior Showmanship is smooth teamwork between you and your dog. This can only be achieved through lots of training and practice at home before you enter a competition.

It is also recommended that you read and study the AKC Junior Showmanship rule book carefully. This booklet covers important topics such as dog ownership and eligibility for competition.

During competition Juniors are required to move their dogs with the rest of the class and present them in a standing position proper for their breed. Then they must move their dogs in a regular judging pattern such as a triangle or an "L" or "T" shape. The judge looks for how well the handlers know basic ring routines, use ring space effectively, and follow directions. They also watch for handlers who make themselves inconspicuous and who present their dogs at their best. A good handler/dog team moves smoothly and in unison. The handler shows off the dog's good points while minimizing any faults.

Competition isn't everything in Junior Showmanship. There are also opportunities to learn good sportsmanship, make new friends, and even develop a possible future career as a handler or breeder. As a Junior Handler, you will meet young people with whom you share a similar interest and can exchange thoughts and ideas. They are competing on the same level as you are, and know the struggles and hardships every Junior Handler faces.

Perhaps you will learn new solutions to old problems through your relationships with others who have spent time in the ring. Basically, Junior Showmanship offers *competition* and *companionship* on a level that will not discourage a young person.

Dogs and Dog Shows

In order to truly understand Junior Showmanship, it is necessary to have a working knowledge of dogs and dog shows.

Domestic dogs descended from their wild ancestors that associated with humans. For centuries, humans have controlled the natural breeding of domesticated dogs. Today, dogs can be produced in any size, shape, color, and even temperament.

Initially, humans bred dogs to meet the needs of home and farm. For example, dogs were bred to ward off intruders; others were bred to herd sheep and cattle; and still others were bred as hunters. To accomplish this, the dogs chosen for breeding were the ones that showed natural tendencies to protect, herd, or hunt. Eventually, people started holding competitions to determine the best hunter or herder among their dogs. The winning dogs were admired for their breeding potential. Organizations were established to provide rules and regulations so that the competitions would be held and judged fairly. These organizations made sure that the dogs in competition were purebred. They also kept a record of pedigrees where each dog's ancestors were written down and properly recorded.

The AKC took on these duties in the United States. Nations all over the world have similar organizations that provide rules for competition and protect the pure breeds of dogs. A purebred dog will produce only dogs exactly like himself. If a mixed breed dog mates with a purebred, the puppies are not true to the purpose for which the breed was originally developed.

As life became easier for humans, dogs were not needed as much for their help as for their companionship. The dog show gradually changed from a competition of skill to a competition of appearance. Breeding dogs became a hobby rather than a means of survival. The parent breed clubs wrote a standard of excellence to tell people how the ideal dog of that breed should look. A judge must be familiar with the variety of dog he is judging to pick the dog that best fits the Standard (description).

Handling purebred dogs in shows has developed into a fine-tuned skill. Some men and women are so good that they become what is known as professional handlers. They make their living by showing other people's dogs in competition.

At first, only very wealthy people could afford to show their dogs. After the industrial revolution, more and more people began to have the time and money to breed and show dogs. Dog shows expanded from a small gathering of the elite on a private country estate, to a community affair, open to the general public.

Eventually, the AKC set up criteria for earning a Championship. A dog must win 15 points in competition, with at least two of the points being major wins under at least two different judges. (From one to five points are awarded. The number is based on the number of dogs of that breed exhibiting at a particular show. A major win is three or more points.) Dogs of many different breeds compete within their breed to obtain points towards the title of Champion. Some of these dogs are handled by professionals, others by amateurs; but they all compete to become Champions.

Let's Spend A Day At The Show

When you go to a dog show, you will see a chaotic jumble of people, dogs, partitions, grooming tables, trophy tables, etc. As your eyes become accustomed to the clutter, you will see that the area is divided into many separate sections, called *rings*. The rings are numbered for easy identification. Each breed of dog entered in the competition that day will be assigned to a specific ring in which to compete. A catalog of events and entries will be available at the superintendent's desk. Purchase a show catalog. In the front you will find a section that notes the ring numbers, the breeds competing in those rings, and the time of day when classes for each breed are scheduled to start. This helps the exhibitor who has entered a dog in the show find out when and where he will be competing.

Suppose we go to Ring 3 and watch the Dalmatian judging. As we leaf through the catalog, we find that Dalmatians are listed in the back under a category called the *Non-Sporting Group*. (For more information on breed groups, see CHAPTER 2; BREED CLASSIFICATIONS section.) Look down the list. Each Dalmatian in competition has been assigned a number. As you glance around, you will see many of the people standing near ringside are wearing arm bands with numbers on them. The number system prevents prejudicial judging based on ownership. The judge never

gets to see the catalog you are holding; he must pick winners based only on the <u>appearance or conformation of the dogs</u>. Arm band numbers on handlers are used so that the judge can write down the winners by number in what is called the *judge's book*. The AKC then correlates the numbers to the dogs entered and awards points accordingly.

As the first Dalmatian and his exhibitor enter the ring, you will see the judge and his helper (the *ring steward*) marking down the dogs that are present in the ring. Points towards a Championship are figured on the basis of how many dogs are present, not on how many were originally entered.

Looking at your catalog, you note that there are several different categories or *classes* of competition for male dogs: Puppy, Novice, American-Bred, Bred by Exhibitor, and Open. There are identical classes for the female dogs, called *bitches*.

Now a Dalmatian puppy and his owner—who is wearing a big grin and carrying a blue ribbon—walk out of the first class. Does this mean that the puppy has won points towards the Champion title? Not yet. There will be a first place-winner in each of the other classes for that breed. Eventually all of these first-place winners will go back into the ring together. All of these first-place-winning male Dalmatians will compete against each other, and only one will be chosen as top winner, or *Winners Dog*. The Winners Dog will be the one to gain points towards the title of Champion. This procedure is followed for all the female Dalmatians until one is chosen as *Winners Bitch*.

How does the judge determine what dog will win first place, or be the top winner? Let's take a look at the judging of the next class of Dalmatians, the Bred by Exhibitor Class. As the exhibitors enter the ring, they stop in a certain spot and place the front and rear feet of their dogs in what's called a *show stance*, or *show position*. The judge watches the dogs carefully, taking mental notes, as they hold this stance.

The judge then motions to the first exhibitor.. All the exhibitors begin to move their dogs around the ring at a slow trot. Again the judge motions to the first exhibitor, who stops where the judge indicates and begins to set his dog's feet in a show stance again. Now the judge looks only at the first dog. He pulls aside the dog's lips to examine his teeth. The judge now feels the texture of the dog's coat, and checks the position of his shoulders, neck, backbone, tail, legs, and chest to examine the dog's physical structure.

Now the judge steps back and says something to the exhibitor, indicating the ring with his hand. The judge has just told the exhibitor to move the dog around the ring in a certain path. What the judge didn't find when he examined the dog with his hands, he may find when he watches the dog move. The basic theory is that when a dog is constructed properly, he will be able to move correctly. The judge looks at things like where the dog places his feet and legs as he moves, whether his movement is smooth and effortless or clumsy and forced. He looks for clean balanced movement, with the legs moving straight ahead in line. It is important that the handler moves the dog in a straight line, neither too slow nor too fast, so that the judge can observe the dog's movement.

Most dogs are bred for some type of work; work requires endurance, and endurance is acquired more efficiently if a dog is structured correctly. Think about your bicycle. Its wheels must be straight, the frame cannot be bent, and the chain must be the right tightness or you will get tired of pedaling. It is the same with a dog. The more effort he has to put into moving his body because of poor structure, the more easily he will tire, and the less work he will be able to do.

Back to the judging in the ring . . .

The judge has just finished examining the last dog in the line and now asks the handlers to move their dogs around the ring as a group. As the dogs trot around the ring, the judge points to the first, second, third, and fourth place winners. These exhibitors and their dogs walk over and stand next to place markers on the ground. Then the judge goes down the line, writing down the exhibitors' arm band numbers in the judge's book. As the judge is handing out ribbons, the next class prepares to go into the ring. Competition proceeds in the same manner for every class. Now, let's watch as the first-place winners of each class of male Dalmatians go back into the ring. The dogs are placed in their show stances, or *stacked*. Again the judge looks each of them over. He may go down the line and check again for eye color, shoulder structure, rear leg structure, or any point that will help him choose one dog over the others as the best male being shown in that breed. He moves them around the ring again, and then we see the judge point to the winner of the Bred-by-Exhibitor Class as the Winners Dog.

But what's this? Another dog and exhibitor are going into the ring to join the first-place winners that are left! Why didn't the others leave the ring and why did another dog and exhibitor join them? Well, the judge is now going to award the ribbon for *Reserve Winners Dog*. This second-place winner in the Bred by Exhibitor Class is held in case something happens to the first-place winner, the Winners Dog. Once in a while the Winners Dog or Winners Bitch will be disqualified. If a disqualification occurs, the points awarded for the win are given to the Reserve Winners.

Finally, there is a class called *Best of Breed*. All the Dalmatians entered in this class are Champions. Why would anyone continue to show a dog once he has become a Champion? There are two reasons. The owner might feel that his dog is a really good example of the breed, and he would like to have other breeders use the dog as a stud dog. A second reason might be that the dog is of such outstanding quality that he is able to compete against Champions of other breeds and possibly win higher honors. By the end of the day, one dog out of all the dogs in the show will be chosen *Best in Show*. This is a very high honor. Only a few Champions become Best in Show dogs. What are the steps to reaching the title of Best of Breed? Let's go back to Ring 3 where the Best of Breed competition is taking place and follow the Dalmatian that wins.

Three Champions are entered in the Best of Breed class, and they are in the ring; but so are the Winners Dog and Winners Bitch. Even though they are not Champions yet, they are allowed to compete against the other Champions because they are the best dog and best bitch in today's competition. It's possible for one of them to win Best of Breed, if the judge feels one of them is a better dog than the Champions.

The judge examines all the dogs in the class and moves them. He points to three of them. They take their places by markers that read "Best of Breed," "Best of Opposite Sex," and "Best of Winners." One of the Champions is awarded the Best of Breed ribbon. The Winners Bitch is awarded the Best of Opposite Sex ribbon; she is also awarded the Best of Winners ribbon.

The *Best of Opposite Sex* title is awarded to a female if the Best of Breed winner is a male, or to a male if the Best of Breed winner is a female. The *Best of Winners* title is awarded to either the Winners Dog or Winners Bitch.

The Best of Breed Dalmatian will now compete against other Best of Breed winners in the Non-Sporting Group. Four ribbons—1st, 2nd, 3rd, and 4th Place—are awarded in each group. When all the groups have been judged, the first-place winners from each of the seven breed groups compete for the title of Best in Show. (For more information on breed groups, see CHAPTER 2; BREED CLASSIFICATIONS section.)

Each level of competition in a dog show gets a little harder as you try for higher honors. Once in a while, you will see a young person, like yourself, competing with his dog in the regular conformation ring and doing his share of winning. However, competition is stiff, and it is easy to become discouraged. Consequently, Junior Showmanship classes have been organized to give young people the opportunity to compete with others at their own experience levels, using a similar procedure as that followed in the regular conformation ring.

Junior Showmanship 🐕

Junior Showmanship is designed to be a fun learning experience. If learning isn't fun for you, then your interest lags; and soon you are not participating, and therefore, not learning.

The majority of clubs that offer Junior Showmanship divide the Class into four sections:

Novice Junior - A class for boys and girls between the ages of 10 and 14 who have not won three first place awards in the Novice Junior Class.

Open Junior - A class for boys and girls between the ages of 10 and 14 who have won three first place awards in the Novice Junior Class.

Novice Senior - A class for boys and girls between the ages of 14 and 18 who have not won three first place awards in the Novice Senior Class.

Open Senior - A class for boys and girls between the ages of 14 and 18 who have won three first place awards in the Novice Senior Class.

At some of the larger AKC shows, the above classes are also divided by sex, although traditionally boys and girls compete together. Additionally, some shows have a *Best Junior Handler* class, where the first-place winners from each class compete with each other for best handler of the day. Anyone between the ages of 10 and 18 can enter a Junior Showmanship competition, as long as he has a Junior Handler number and is in good standing with the AKC. (To obtain a Junior Handler number, contact the AKC Events Records Department at 212-696-8281/8282/8283.) Additionally, the dog he is showing must be a registered purebred, which either the junior handler or a member of his family owns. (See APPENDIX II on how to register your dog with the AKC.) The AKC rule book states that each "dog must be owned by the Junior Handler or by the Junior Handler's father, mother, brother, sister, aunt, uncle, grandfather, or grandmother, including the corresponding step and half relations." There are no other restrictions.

LIMITED CLASSES

Once in a while, you may see Limited Junior Showmanship classes in the premium list. Limited classes require you to have a certain number of wins from other shows before you can enter. The prestigious Westminster Kennel Club Show in New York City, held in February of each year, is an example of Limited Junior Showmanship classes. To enter Westminster, you must have eight first place wins in the Open Class earned any time between January 1 and December 31 of the previous year.

Other dog shows throughout the United States offer Limited Junior Showmanship classes, but their requirements are usually lower than those for Westminster—perhaps only one or two previous wins from the Open Class are required.

AWARDS

Each Junior Showmanship class has four place winners. Once a handler receives three first-place ribbons in a Novice Class, he or she may automatically enter the Open Class, even that same day.

As mentioned before, some shows will have the first-place winners in each class compete with each other for the Best Junior Handler award, which is an award similar to the Best in Show award for conformation classes. If a Junior Handler wins his or her third first-place ribbon in Novice Class at one of these shows and decides to compete in the Open Class at that show and does not win first place, he or she is not eligible to compete for Best Junior Handler. Handlers must be undefeated in a particular show to compete for Best Junior Handler. Winning isn't everything—Junior Showmanship is fun as well as educational.

Many clubs give trophies (along with ribbons) to the winners. In addition, some national and local breed clubs have a Best Junior Handler of the Year award. Junior Handlers receive point awards for each placement in a class. A certain number of points are awarded on the basis of how many other Juniors are in competition that day. (This point system is similar to that found in the conformation ring.) The highest point-winning junior in a given year is then awarded Best Junior Handler.

As you can see, there will always be a higher goal to achieve in Junior Showmanship. Winning is not the main reason for competing in these classes, but it is a nice reward for all the hard work. More importantly, you will learn that your dog is a creature that thinks and feels, much like yourself. You will learn to read his signals and attempts to communicate, as he will learn to read you. You will learn to work as a team with your dog, learn sportsmanship, and will have the opportunity to meet and communicate with exhibitors your own age, expanding your circle of friends to a national or even international level. You will gain knowledge of the world of dogs and be able to communicate with adults on this topic. Furthermore, you will have grown beyond what you would have ever thought possible.

Pets by Paulette

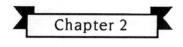

Chapter 2

Choosing A Dog

Obviously you cannot go far in junior showmanship without a dog! If you are fortunate, you will be able to borrow a dog from your parents or another relative who is already active in showing dogs. Often circumstance determines the breed of dog you will handle. Perhaps your parents are active in breeding dogs, so they keep a puppy especially for you to show. Perhaps you have become friends with a professional handler who knows someone who would place a puppy with you, if you will agree to show it. A few of you will be very lucky and your parents will buy you a puppy. Which breed will you choose?

If you have a choice, take the time to go to a few dog shows to observe the Junior Showmanship classes. (It's a good idea for anyone interested in handling to first be a spectator.) You will learn what is expected of you and your dog. You will also see that no one breed wins more than another breed. Remember, it is the handling ability of the Junior that is being judged, not the dog.

Which Dog For You?

Nevertheless, a few words of wisdom may save you some heartaches later. First, keep in mind the physical aspects of particular breeds. Pick a breed with size and temperament that will fit into your family's lifestyle. For example, if you are interested in choosing a Great Dane or Irish Wolfhound, think about how large he will be at maturity. This wouldn't be an appropriate dog if you live in an apartment. Large dogs need lots of room to grow and exercise.

Also consider your size in relationship to the dog's size. If you are small, you may not be able to control a large dog, or you may have to race at an unattractive pace to keep ahead of him. If your dog quickly becomes too strong for you to handle and train, both of you are going to wear out your welcome at home. On the other hand, toy breeds are placed on a grooming table for the judge's examination. Are you able to lift your dog in this manner?

If you are large and not as well coordinated as you would like, you may look better with a medium or large breed. Some of the hunting breeds are shown in full extension when presented to the judge, which requires you to fully extend your dog's body from head to tail. Are your arms long enough to do this?

Second, a breed's personality is important, too. Do you want an active or a relatively quiet dog? Do you want a dog loyal to one person (yourself) or many people? Can you control a dog from one of the more active or aggressive breeds? In Junior Showmanship, you and your dog should appear as a well-coordinated team. The dog should respond to your cues and look alert, sparkling, and under control. Of course, once you get to know your new dog, you will find that he has his own distinct personality within the general characteristics of the breed. Once you choose a breed, look for a puppy with an outgoing temperament and one that responds to you. You will probably feel an almost immediate attachment to the right puppy.

Third, be honest with yourself about how much time you are able to devote to your new dog. Quite possibly working with a dog you plan to show will take time away from other activities. Plan for feeding and training alone to take an hour a day. With this in mind, can you afford to spend another hour or two a day on grooming? If not, then you would be wise to choose a breed that has few grooming requirements, such as a short-haired breed. ALL breeds need grooming of one kind or another, but the long-haired breeds need their coats combed or brushed every day in order to look their best in the ring. Terriers and Poodles need various combinations of stripping, clipping, and scissoring. Setters have feathered leg and tail hair that needs constant combing and trimming. Even the short-haired breeds need to be brushed occasionally. ALL breeds need their nails clipped on a regular basis. So, it is important that you know what is involved with grooming a particular breed of dog before you choose it. Most breeders are happy to answer questions about their dogs if you ask for the information.

Ultimately, there is no governing rule in Junior Showmanship about what breed of dog a boy or girl can take into the ring. It is how you present the dog that is important, and that will ultimately depend on how much work you put into your own and your dog's training.

Breed Classifications

The following American Kennel Club (AKC) breed classification descriptions may be helpful in choosing a breed that is right for you. The general AKC breed classifications are:

SPORTING GROUP

This group represents the breeds that assist humans in game hunting. The various breeds in this group are bred to help hunters by setting up and retrieving game. Their ability to use their noses, along with their capability to retrieve and flush game, has helped humans provide food for their families over centuries. Today, these friendly breeds are popular companions and favorite household pets. They are also an active bunch; and consequently need proper room for exercise.

HOUND GROUP

This group, unlike the Sporting Group, is bred to hunt for themselves. They have either sensitive noses or acute eyesight; with some breeds having both traits. The hound group is divided into *Scent Hounds* and *Gaze Hounds*. They are athletic and especially swift; and consequently require a great deal of exercise. Some of the oldest domestic dogs are in this group. People have used their hunting skills for centuries. They are, more often than not, one-person dogs.

WORKING GROUP

These dogs assist humans in guarding property, hauling carts, and protecting against intruders. Consisting mostly of large breeds, this group needs a large yard or plenty of exercise. Many of today's more popular breeds exist in this group, such as the Doberman Pinscher and Rottweiler.

HERDING GROUP

As the name implies, breeds in this group assist humans in herding livestock. Like the working breeds, they also are protectors of home, farm, and family. Today, as in the past, you will find many of these breeds herding flocks of sheep, cattle, and even goats. Room to grow is an essential need with these breeds, as they are bred to work and need exercise.

TERRIER GROUP

Originally known as "Earth Dogs of the Hunt," these breeds were skilled in burrowing and catching small game from their underground homes. There are many variations in this group: short legs and long legs; rough coats and smooth coats; and many colors of hair coat. Terrier breeds carry a certain amount of "fire," their energy levels are always high, and they make wonderful companion animals and house dogs. They are often "characters." Exuding gameness, they can be funny, determined aggressors, or charming clowns. Most terrier breeds require lots of grooming.

TOY GROUP

These compact little dogs are appropriately named and make wonderful house pets for a small home or apartment. They are sometimes called *"lap dogs"* or *"ladies' pets."* They have diverse breed characteristics. Today, most of the toy breeds are companions, unlike the other groups that still perform some of the tasks they were originally bred to do.

NON-SPORTING GROUP

This is the most difficult group to define because of its diversity. Originally, some of these breeds assisted humans in various types of work. The Poodle was originally a retriever. The Schipperke was bred to guard canal boats. But their functions have ceased to exist today; consequently, they are referred to as non-sporting dogs. Other breeds are in this group because they do not fit in any other group. So, this group is a hodgepodge of breeds with significant variations in shape, size, origination and purpose.

Each group has its share of short- and long-haired breeds. You should think about the time needed to properly groom each breed. Although Junior Showmanship judges will not judge on your dog's breed characteristics, you must present him in the best possible way in comparison to his breed standard. Judges will note whether a handler has made an effort to prepare his dog for the ring. So, do not select a dog that requires stripping or clipping if you don't have the interest or time to learn to do it right.

Perhaps most important of all, you must LIKE the breed you choose. If there is no attraction to or love for the breed, you will soon tire of Junior Showmanship. Being a living creature, your dog will always require your care, regardless of whether you compete with him. Remember, all puppies are cute, but they all grow up and require care and attention. Look at it from the dog's point of view. Select the breed you think would be the happiest with you and your environment. A happy dog is a joy to have around.

One final word — your new puppy will also have to fit in at home. So, make sure you discuss everything thoroughly with your parents. Ideally, you will be totally responsible for your dog and his training. Having your mom or dad feed, train, or assume responsibility for your dog is NOT the idea of Junior Showmanship. Becoming a pet's caretaker is not a short-term undertaking. The life span of most dogs is eight to twelve years. You are responsible for your dog's life during this time; and he is dependent on you to take care of him.

So, in choosing a dog that's right for you, think carefully, take your time, and study the different breeds. Your local library is a good place to begin your research of the various breeds. When you're ready to choose your dog, the American Kennel Club can direct you to breeders, clubs, and shows in your area.

Judith Strom

Chapter 3

Getting Your Dog Ready To Show

Once you have a dog to work with, you will need to learn the basic handling techniques common to all breeds. Do this BEFORE you are ready to enter the ring for the first time. Once you have this foundation, you'll be able to learn much more, much faster. Of course, learning the basics takes time and practice. So, again, consider your decision carefully before you jump into this sport.

If possible, sign up for some handling lessons. Professional handlers and show-giving clubs usually give lessons on basic show handling techniques. If this isn't possible, ask a professional handler if you could watch and listen to a lesson; then go home and practice what you saw. These lessons will give you a good idea of what it's like to be in the ring with your dog.

You can also attend *Fun Matches*, which are practices that help prepare both handlers and dogs for real shows. And, as mentioned previously, you can attend an AKC show and observe Junior Handlers in action.

You will also have to learn some specific pointers about how your particular breed is shown. There are basic handling moves common to all breeds. Each breed also has certain handling characteristics of its own. If you are not exactly sure how to show your breed properly, seek help from someone who does know. One source of information is a professional handler. Look for a handler who shows your breed of dog. Polish your manners, gather up your courage, and approach him or her while they are grooming or standing at ringside. Never try to talk to an exhibitor just as they are getting ready to go in the ring. If you explain who you are and what you need to know, the handler will probably be happy to help you.

Another person to ask is a breeder. Breeders can be extremely helpful sources of information, especially for newcomers to the sport of dogs. The breeder you purchased your dog from will be the best source of information. Breeders are proud of their puppies and delighted to help you show the dog to its best advantage. Further sources of information are people who show the same breed. Many of them have spent several years learning about the breed and enjoy talking about a subject they know well.

You will find many of them willing to help you learn to show your dog correctly.

Your Dog's Health

Every dog will need medical care from time to time. If he is to give you his best at all times, he must be healthy. Unlike a human, your dog cannot tell you when he is not feeling well. He needs routine checkups by a veterinarian. You must also check your dog for parasites, fleas, ticks, and other pests. Your puppy will have to be immunized against certain diseases that can kill dogs. Choose a good veterinarian and ask him to advise you of the required shots, test your dog for parasites and give you suggestions on care and feeding.

Learn to trust your veterinarian. He will become an important part of your dog's life. Once you have chosen a vet, don't change without a good reason. Like human doctors, veterinarians get to know their patients and will soon learn your dog's special needs and personality quirks. A vet who has gotten to know your dog through routine visits is well prepared to deal with him in an emergency.

As a responsible dog owner, here are some important things you need to know about your dog:

• A dog's normal temperature is 101.5 degrees Fahrenheit.

• Dogs may get tiny ear mites in their ear canal, where the parasites multiply and infect their ears. Clean your dog's ears frequently. Your veterinarian can explain how to clean your dog's ears and how to recognize these parasites.

• Worms of various types are internal parasites that can sap strength from your dog and make him irritable and unhappy. When you take him in for his regular shots, take a sample of his stool from that morning—your vet will test it to make sure he is free of parasites. If your dog begins to lose his coat, lose weight, or show other signs of ill health, get a stool check done immediately.

• *Heartworm* is a parasite that spreads through the bloodstream, settling in the heart and clogging the arteries. Mosquitoes carry this disease. It is deadly if not treated. Follow your vet's suggestions as to preventive measures, testing, and/or treatment.

• Diarrhea is sometimes a sign of ill health, but it can also be an indication that your dog has eaten something odd. Watch him carefully, and if his bout of runny stools doesn't pass in a day, call your vet immediately.

The main thing to remember is that your vet is invaluable to your dog's good health. Work with him to keep your dog healthy.

Grooming

As mentioned previously, it's important to consider a breed's grooming needs before you choose your new dog. The breed books available today cover specific grooming requirements. Read about your breed and understand the demands asked of you. Don't count on your parents to do this for you. Remember, Junior Handling is a project that you chose to undertake, and you should take full responsibility for it.

You can probably get the best grooming tips from your dog's breeder. Also, you can attend a dog show and observe your breed being groomed in the designated grooming areas. Never get in anyone's way or hold anyone up before they go into the ring. Be sure to ask if a person has time to talk to you first. If not, ask that person if it would be possible to come back after their breed (and yours) has been judged in the conformation ring. They might have more time to answer your grooming questions.

Reading, asking, and observing will be your best teachers, but practice will be your best answer. Once you know your breed's grooming needs, start collecting your own set of grooming tools. Many of these tools are inexpensive enough that you can purchase them with allowance money or other funds. Before you decide which grooming tools to purchase, however, observe what tools other people use to groom your breed of dog. Also talk to them about which methods they prefer, what techniques they use, and where to purchase certain tools.

In addition, you'll need a grooming case or container in which to carry your tools. You may want to ask for a special grooming case as a birthday gift. Otherwise, you can use your dad's old brief case, a metal tool box, or a box from the hardware store. Standard grooming boxes are sold at dog shows.

Stock your grooming case first with basic supplies that are common to all breeds:

- small, blunt-tipped scissors for whisker and hair trimming
- nail clippers or grinders
- cotton swabs for ear cleaning
- shampoo
- spare towel for rainy day shows
- show collar and show lead
- hair brush and/or comb
- spray-on coat cleaner for last minute touchup

You probably have some additional items in mind already. Having your own tools will make the job easier and save you much time.

To insure the best results for your grooming efforts, select a spot to do your grooming that is out of everyone's way. Choose a place that your parents approve of, that is well-lighted, and that allows you to hold onto your dog easily. Get everything you are going to need for grooming assembled ahead of time.

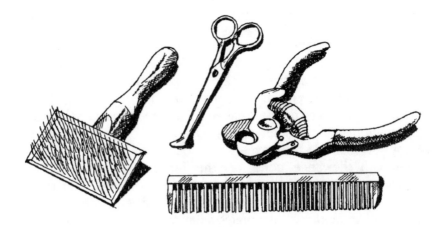

If your family is already active with dogs, you may own a grooming table. If not, try to find an area in your house that is roomy and comfortable for your dog. Always use the same place so that your dog will realize that this spot means the business of grooming and will behave accordingly. Your dog may not like it the first few times you put him on the grooming table. Look at it from his point of view. He is up high and tied to one spot, and a human is doing strange things to his body. If you keep these things in mind, you will have more patience when he misbehaves while you're trying to groom him. Talk to your dog in a friendly, soothing voice. Praise him when he cooperates. Take this opportunity to run your hands over his body, quickly checking for burrs, mats, cuts, scratches, ticks, injuries, or anything else that doesn't belong there. Your touch will comfort the dog.

It is impossible to give specific pointers about grooming all the breeds used in Junior Showmanship. Therefore, the following descriptions comprise the three steps in the dog grooming process that are common to almost every breed.

1. CLEANING THE DOG

Always bathe a short-haired dog the day before a show. Some long-haired breeds don't require a total bath each time they are shown; there are grooming aids available that freshen a dog's coat as you spray and brush.

Check with your parents before using the tub or kitchen sink for bathing your dog. Collect some old bath towels and your dog's shampoo. There are a variety of shampoos available; be sure to choose one suited to your dog's type of hair coat. Next, wet your dog down thoroughly in comfortable warm water—not so hot it burns him, or so cold it chills him. Apply the shampoo, lather, scrub him thoroughly with your fingers, and then rinse. Usually one soaping is enough, unless he's been frolicking in the mud. Be careful not to get water or soap in or near your dog's eyes, as you can give him an eye infection. Wash your dog's face much like you wash your own face, being careful not to get soap in his eyes, ears, mouth, and nose. Try putting cotton balls in his ears to keep water from getting into his ear canal.

Rinse your dog thoroughly. Be sure to get all the soap out of his coat and off his skin. Soap on the coat attracts dirt when it dries and can feel sticky to the touch. Soap on the skin causes dry skin or dandruff, and can cause hair to fall out.

Turn off the water when you are sure the dog is free of soap residue. You may want to squeeze some of the water out of his coat by hand before toweling him. Then gently press the towels to his body rather than briskly rubbing, or rub gently in the direction that the hair grows. When the dog is as dry as possible, take him out of the tub.

Now, be sure your dog doesn't get chilled. Keep him active and in a relatively warm area. His own body heat will help him dry off quickly. If you have a long-haired breed, you can dry his hair with a hair dryer set on low or medium heat. (Check before you borrow one from a family member.) Take your time fluffing and drying your dog's hair. He may be frightened at first, but he will soon get used to the noise and the feel of the hot air.

Note: Be sure to clean up the area you used to wash your dog. This will help keep the other members of your home happy.

2. TRIMMING THE NAILS

Keep your show dog's toenails as short as possible. This is going to be the challenge of your career! A nail that is too long will make it difficult for your dog to move properly, and his feet may even begin to hurt. Cutting a nail too short is painful for your dog, and he may become touchy and difficult for you to trim later. If you cut too deep into the quick of the nail, it will bleed. Consequently, this is an important skill to master.

If you cannot hear little "click-click" sounds as your dog moves across a hard-surface floor, then his nails are nice and short. To keep them this way, you will have to trim them about every two weeks. Some breeders recommend using clippers (similar to scissors); others recommend a motorized grinding tool.

A grinding tool is more difficult to use, but there is less chance of cutting into the *quick*. The quick is a painfully sensitive portion of flesh underlying a dog's nail. If you hold one of your dog's nails up to the light, you can see this pink center area that contains the nerves and blood vessels. If you cut into this area, your dog will more than likely yelp in pain and the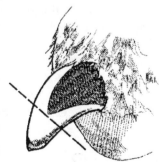

nail will begin to bleed. After too many such accidents, your dog will not trust you to clip his nails or even want you to hold his paw. So, find a quiet place to work on your dog's nails, and take your time trimming them.

3. TRIMMING THE WHISKERS

Whisker trimming is much easier than nail trimming. Begin by purchasing a pair of manicure scissors with blunt or rounded tips at your local drugstore. NEVER use pointed scissors around your dog's face, as you might poke him in the eyes. Dogs can jerk their heads much faster than you can react, and your dog might get a pair of scissors in his face before you realize it.

Select an area with good light, take your dog's muzzle in your hand, and begin to snip his whiskers one at a time at the skin line. Move his muzzle about in the light to be sure you trimmed all his whiskers. Dogs have a sneaky trick of folding their whiskers back against their muzzle so that you think you have finished trimming. Then they pop the remaining whisker stubs out with a little gleam in their eyes, as if so say, "Surprise! Got you!"

Trim wild eyebrow hairs and cheek and chin whiskers in the same manner. Almost all breeds are shown with clean muzzles, or muzzles free of whiskers. You can check with other handlers to make sure that your breed is supposed to be shown with the whiskers trimmed.

A FEW SPECIAL NOTES ON GROOMING

Working with long-haired breeds requires much more than just a simple bath and a nail and whisker trim. As stated before, it's important that you have a full understanding about the grooming involved before you choose a long-haired dog as a pet. Professional handlers make grooming long-haired dogs look easy, but remember that they have been grooming for a long time and are able to combine their craftsmanship and speed. Visit a local grooming shop to get an idea about the work involved with grooming a specific long-haired dog. Professional groomers aren't working to get dogs ready for the show ring, but you'll be able to see them use some of the same grooming methods and techniques. When you visit a professional groomer, you'll also be able to see how the groomer uses a grooming table. It's important for you to learn how to use a grooming table properly, as it's easy for your dog to get hurt if you're not careful. For example, NEVER, NEVER LEAVE YOUR DOG WHEN HE IS TIED TO A GROOMING TABLE. He's your pal and will try to jump down to follow you, if you go away. This could be fatal, as he might hang himself or break his neck.

Practice grooming your dog just as you would practice training him. A good Junior Handler should be able to do everything necessary to get his dog ready for the show ring, just as he does everything necessary once he is in the ring. Once you have learned as much as you can about Junior Showmanship and you begin to enter shows, getting your dog ready for competition will become second nature. Take time the day before the show to do all the little things your breed requires. Leave nothing for the day of the show except final touchups. Waiting until the last minute before you enter the ring can upset both you and your dog. You will both perform better if grooming is done at home in the familiar atmosphere of the grooming area and not at ringside the day of the show.

Never take an ungroomed dog into the ring. One of the things the judge will be looking for is evidence that you have taken the time to care for your dog properly. There is a saying, "If you can't stand the heat, get out of the kitchen!" If you don't like the chores of grooming, then maybe you should look into another sport. The amount of time you spent working with your dog at home is usually evident when you walk into the ring. Ninety-five percent of Junior Handler award winners work with their dogs at home. The other five percent have just been lucky . . . so far.

I have mentioned several grooming points in this section. Hopefully, you won't feel overwhelmed. As a beginner, there is a lot to learn, but grooming can also be fun. It is an opportunity to be with your dog and to help him feel or look his best. If you are working with a new puppy or an older dog that has not been groomed before, start slowly. The process of grooming is new to both of you, and you must not rush it. Go slowly, learning as you go, and when either of you gets tired or frustrated, quit. Never push yourself or your dog beyond this point. You can always come back and finish the task later.

Grooming is an art, and you certainly won't learn it overnight. Observe others and ask many questions. Of course, your own hands-on experience is your best teacher. If you can, learn under the direction of an experienced groomer, letting them direct you step by step. You will be amazed at how quickly you pick up tips to make your dog look magnificent. A good groomer will even teach you little tricks to help your dog's ear or tail set, enhance your dog's expression, and minimize structural faults.

Judith Strom

Chapter 4

Preparing For Competition

Training both yourself and your dog is the most important aspect of Junior Showmanship. Without training you won't be likely to win an award. It takes a well-trained dog to stand in the ring for such a long time during a competition and perform as expected. If carefully followed, the training hints in this section will help you to win those first-place ribbons.

For starters, it's essential to know the physical structure of your dog to be an effective trainer. You will find many of these terms referred to in dog breed standards, and when you are asked to stack or gait your dog, these terms may sometimes be used. Study the following illustrations and other references given in the back of this book.

The information in this section will be valuable to you whether you are training a new puppy, an untrained dog, or a partially trained puppy or adult dog. Always start from the beginning when you're working with a dog that's new to you.

The key to training dogs successfully lies in working for short periods of time while you and your dog are in a happy mood. Two fifteen-minute sessions each day are ideal. During these sessions, you will ask your dog to hold a show stance or stacked position for progressively longer periods of time. Also, you must accustom him to having his body and teeth examined.

When you first take your dog into the ring, it's going to be a new experience for him. He may be distracted by all the other dogs. If you don't prepare him ahead of time, he will not know how to handle this new situation. He will begin to misbehave in the ring, and you will lose patience with each other.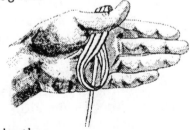

Show Leads

You will need to choose a suitable show lead for your dog. This lead should give you maximum control over your dog, while being easy for you to keep folded in the palm of your hand.

NEVER use a lead so big or so long that it keeps falling out of your hand and dangling down on your dog.

There are many different varieties of show leads. Check with breeders of your specific breed of dog to see what type of lead they recommend. Toy breeds use a different type of lead than larger breeds; and medium-sized breeds have the largest choice of all. The following text describes the various types of show leads.

THE SLIP LEAD

This lead is used mostly for smaller dogs and dogs that do not need a great deal of control. It adjusts to the size of a dog's neck by sliding a tight-fitting bead or rubber ring down to his neck.

THE MARTINGALE

This is a combination slip lead and choker, used for most medium-sized dogs. It has a choke-type collar with a ring for the lead to slip through and a sliding bead to tighten everything into place. It gives much better control for an energetic dog, and the chances of a dog slipping out of the martingale are minimal.

THE CHOKER AND LEASH

The choker portion of this lead is a fine metal chain similar to the type used in obedience work. The leash is cotton and has a snap at one end. This lead is used differently than the chain choke collar and leather leash used in obedience work. It affords maximum control, if used properly.

Whichever types of lead you use, remember to keep it under your dog's chin, RIGHT BEHIND HIS EARS. If you cannot handle the choker and leash gracefully, stick with a slip lead or martingale. Keep the lead folded neatly in the palm of your hand at all times. If it has too much bulk and keeps slipping out of your grasp, consider switching to either a thinner or a shorter lead. Never let the lead dangle out of your hand to distract the judge's eye.

Watch how some handlers wind their leads up and tuck them into their left hands. Practice this until it becomes easy for you to do, too. There will be times when you must quickly shift the lead from your left hand to your right hand and back again. This is easy if you have the lead folded correctly.

Lead Training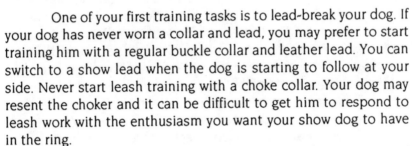

One of your first training tasks is to lead-break your dog. If your dog has never worn a collar and lead, you may prefer to start training him with a regular buckle collar and leather lead. You can switch to a show lead when the dog is starting to follow at your side. Never start leash training with a choke collar. Your dog may resent the choker and it can be difficult to get him to respond to leash work with the enthusiasm you want your show dog to have in the ring.

Begin by accustoming the dog to the feel of the show lead around his neck and to pressure from the lead. This is going to take time. *Don't try to force your dog to cooperate.* Most dogs have minds of their own and only respond when <u>they</u> are ready. Initially, short but frequent sessions will be the most productive. Your dog has a short attention span and gets bored easily, especially if you are trying to get him to do something he doesn't want to do.

You will have the most success in your training if you always approach your dog with a spirit of fun. Put the show lead around his neck, RIGHT BEHIND HIS EARS, and let him get used to how it feels. Let your dog play, bite, and romp at first. He will soon get bored with playing with the lead, and you can then progress to guiding him around with it. <u>Never</u> pull your dog around by the lead; use it only to <u>guide</u> him.

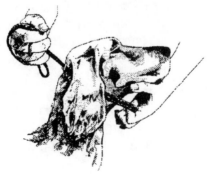

With the lead around his neck and play time over, begin to walk at your dog's side, talking to him encouragingly. Call him by name, praise him, and keep a happy tone in your voice. Try to get him to take a few steps along with you. If he doesn't cooperate at first, take off the lead and put it away for a few hours. Cuddle him, love him, and let him know he is a good dog. Later, try again until he realizes that you want him to walk beside you when you move away. Never scold him if he isn't cooperative; always praise him when he is doing well. The last thing you want him to associate with the show lead is someone who scolds, yells, and demands perfection. If you react this way every time your dog does not cooperate on the show lead, he will begin to hate it. It is embarrassing to drag your dog into the ring all hunched over with his tail between his legs just because he has learned to hate the show lead and everything associated with it.

If, as an adult, your dog begins to drag his heels at the sight of the show lead, take a hint from professional handlers. They will take a dog that is acting like this, put the show lead on him, and then do nothing but play gently with him, using a happy voice to give lots of praise. Continue this attitude training until the dog perks up. If you watch top handlers in the conformation ring at a dog show, you will see that they seldom discipline their dogs—they coax them skillfully into performing desired actions.

When your dog begins to cooperate on the show lead, take time to do the following little experiment. Place the lead around your dog's neck, RIGHT BEHIND HIS EARS. (See the previous illustration.) For a minute, let the lead slip down until it's at the bottom of his neck by his shoulders. Now try to lead him around. Doesn't work as well, does it? You really have to pull on the lead to keep any sort of guiding control over your dog's actions. Now, place it up around his ears again. Tighten it and stand in front of your dog, looking down at him with the lead in your hands. Then put the lead in your left hand and gently pull to the left. See his body begin to lean? Then see him move his feet to get his balance back? Now gently pull to the right. The same things will happen in reverse. Notice that it doesn't take any strength at all on your part to get your dog to sway to the left or right.

This knowledge will prove more valuable during the next stage of your training when you need to move your dog a step or two in one direction or another. That's why it's important to keep the show lead up around your dog's neck, RIGHT BEHIND HIS EARS!

When your dog is used to the feel of the lead around his neck and follows you willingly, you can begin to vary the pace at which you move with your dog. Get him used to moving at a fast trot or *show gait*. Work with him until he can control his desire to break into an all-out run. Then you can use your knowledge of lead control to guide him into a left or right turn as you are moving. Always move with your dog on your left side and the show lead in your left hand.

To guide your dog into a left turn, extend your left arm with the show lead in your left hand so that it is straight out from the side of your body. This movement should pull your dog to his left, and he will begin to turn in that direction to keep his balance. To help guide him, you may also want to put your right hand under his chin and gently turn his head to the left. His body should follow through with a left turn.

Use the same sort of guidance to help him into a right turn, but <u>keep the lead in your left hand</u>. You will simply extend your arm again, but move your lead to the right firmly but without jerking. You may want to use the chin guidance method here as well. The main caution is DO NOT JERK the lead. First, it can be painful. Second, it will cause your dog to break his stride and look awkward in his movement. Your main goal is to achieve a smooth, fluid movement, executing turns without a break in stride. Also, don't forget to use your voice, as it is an important tool to use in movement training.

Stacking

Once your dog is responding fairly well to the lead you can begin to teach him about stacking. *Stacking* means setting each leg in the position most fitting for the breed. It is also called the *show stance*.

Initially, your main concern is teaching your dog to leave his feet where you put them. Start by taking one or two sessions just to handle your dog's front legs. To do this, stand over your dog. Run your left hand up and down his left shoulder, picking up his left leg and putting it back down while lifting his chin gently with your right hand. Try to do this with a preoccupied air, not speaking to him at all. If you have been talking constantly throughout your lessons until now, this new attitude might confuse him, and he may quietly stand there in puzzlement.

If you can get your dog to be quiet for fifteen to thirty seconds while you are doing this, stop the lesson and praise and play with him. Then go back to this lesson later in the day and repeat it. Work only with the front legs at first, until he begins to realize that you want him to leave his feet where you put them. Praise the slightest bit of cooperation, even if it lasts for a few seconds. Your dog will begin to keep his feet still for longer and longer periods as he matures and as his awareness of what you want increases.

Remember, each breed of dog has a unique show stance. You will need to consult your breeder or another source to find your dog's correct stance. Some stacking procedures are common to all breeds. So, let's practice some of the common movements.

Start by taking the show lead—which is around your dog's neck—in your right hand. Gently guide your dog so he is sideways in front of your body. His head will be close to your right arm; his rear will be near your left arm. In the show ring, the judge usually begins by looking at your dog's left side, so you must get used to starting from this position.

Now gather the show lead into your right hand so that none of it dangles down to distract your dog. Keep your right hand just below his chin. (See Illustration.)

Then, lean over him and grasp his left front leg just below the elbow. Lift his leg slightly and gently turn it to the right and then to the left. See how much control you have over his leg? Now grasp his leg down by his paw and try the same thing. Doesn't work, does it? So, the elbow is the correct place to begin setting your dog's leg.

Next, lift his leg slightly off the ground, turn it gently until his paw is pointing straight ahead, and place his leg back on the floor. It's helpful to practice in front of a mirror when you are standing over your dog because it allows you to see when you are placing his leg in the correct position.

Keeping the lead gathered in a bunch, transfer it to your left hand. Crouch down in front of your dog. You are now ready to set his right front leg. Grasp his right front leg at the elbow with your right hand and follow the same procedure as you did for his left leg. Always keep a firm hold on the show lead while you are placing your dog's feet so he knows you are still in control of the situation.

Hint: If you keep your dog's head facing straight ahead, it will be easier to keep his feet pointing straight ahead as well. As you learned earlier, your dog's feet will tend to follow the direction of his head. So, if his head turns to the right while you are placing his feet, his feet will have a tendency to turn to the right as well.

During the first week or two of lessons, concentrate more on encouraging your dog to keep his front feet where you have placed them. Do not worry whether you have placed them in the correct position. Your dog will soon consider this procedure familiar and will keep his feet where you put them, allowing you to focus more attention on correct foot placement.

When your dog has learned to keep his front feet in place, try transferring the show lead from your left hand back into your right hand. Tell your dog to stay while you gently stroke his neck and shoulders. Gradually increase the time you ask him to hold this position until he can stand still for a minute or more without moving his feet out of place. Always praise him lavishly in a happy tone of voice when he cooperates.

After one or two weeks of short training sessions, your dog should leave his front feet where you place them for progressively longer periods of time. Now you are ready to begin handling his rear legs.

Use the same introduction to this new lesson as you did with the front legs. This skill will probably take less time to master, as your dog will now be used to having his legs handled and placed.

To set your dog's left rear leg, fold the leash up tight and hold it in your right hand. Reach <u>under</u> your dog's body with your left hand and grasp his left hock. Place your thumb towards the inside of your dog's leg and your fingers around the outside of his leg. Lift gently and push against his hock with your thumb; just a slight pressure will cause the lower leg to swivel left or right. Use this method to make sure his rear paw is pointing straight ahead when you set it down again. Set his right rear leg in the same way, with your <u>left hand</u>. There is no need to switch hands on the lead when setting his rear legs.

Do not stretch your dog's rear legs way out behind him. The stretching might cause him to lose his balance because this is not his natural stance. In addition, he may not be able to take the strain. The key to placing any breed's rear legs is to handle the legs by the hocks to get maximum control when setting the legs.

Note: Toy breeds are too close to the ground to reach under their bodies, so you can set their rear legs by grasping their hocks from behind.

The profile of your dog should be elegant. Correct leg handling and placement will assure that his legs are not bunched up under him, nor his rear stretched nearly horizontal. His hocks should be perpendicular to the ground when viewed from the side, and parallel to each other when viewed from behind. His rear paws should be placed just slightly farther apart than his front paws.

At first, just practice stacking your dog squarely and teach him that you want him to stay put. When he is willing, you can begin stacking him in his correct show stance.

Accepting The Judge's Examination

Another important aspect of your dog's training is to accustom him to having his teeth inspected and his mouth handled by strangers. This can be a family project, if your family is willing to cooperate. Ask everyone in your family to handle your dog's lips, raising them enough to expose his teeth. They do not need to know the correct procedure for a bite examination because they are merely trying to help you get your dog used to having his mouth handled. Ask them to reach down and lift your dog's lips every time they see him. Also ask them to pet and praise your dog for allowing them to handle his mouth. If enough people take a second or two each day to handle your dog's mouth, eventually he will accept it without objection. He'll probably be thinking to himself, "Oh, it's just another nutty human pulling at my lips again!"

It's important to reassure your dog that you mean him no harm when you examine his teeth and mouth. A dog knows instinctively that he must protect his teeth and mouth from injury or his survival will be threatened. Giving your dog a food reward for allowing his mouth to be handled might encourage his cooperation. Just be sure he doesn't become dependent on that treat or he might not perform in the ring without it.

Another way your family can help you in your training is by examining your dog the way the judge would while he is stacked in his show stance. Ask them to run their hands down his neck and shoulders, over his back, and down his legs. If your dog is a male, he also needs to get used to having his testicles handled. His instinct will be to protect this sensitive area. Once again, time, patience, and encouragement will help him to overcome his natural fears. While your dog is being examined, you'll want him to remain just as you positioned him.

The more you practice training now, the better you will be later in the Junior Showmanship ring. When you are in the ring, you will need to move around your dog while he remains in a stacked position. So, the more time you put into training him to hold his show pose while you are moving around him now, the better he will perform in the ring later.

The goal of all this training is to make a team out of handler and dog. With proper training, you should eventually be able to set your dog's feet in the right position, and your well-trained dog will leave his feet just where you put them.

After a couple of weeks of training your dog to follow your lead and cooperate by holding the stacked position, you will find that each new step becomes a little easier than the last one. This will not only take training, but also much love, praise, and support. You dog will never follow you happily at your heels, with his eyes sparkling and his tail wagging, if you yell, scream, scold, hit, or otherwise make him feel miserable. Would you spend much time around someone who made you feel like that? No! Everyone wants to feel loved and accepted, including your dog. If you treat him right, he'll work his heart out for you.

This dog is gaiting happily on a slack lead.

Photo by Kent Dannen

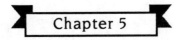

Chapter 5

How To Enter A Show

When you feel that you and your dog are sufficiently trained, you'll want to enter your first show. This section will help explain all the necessary forms you'll need to fill out and how to do it. It will also give you some tips on such things as proper dress and good sportsmanship.

When a local kennel club decides to give a show, they send out what is called a *premium list*. It gives the name, date, and location of the show; any prizes offered; the classes; and a list of the judges. Official American Kennel Club (AKC) entry blanks are included. You must always use one of these when entering any AKC approved show.

A copy of a current entry blank, both front and back is shown below. Noted in all capital letters in the following text are the sections that you will need to fill out when you enter an AKC show.

The name of the kennel club giving the show is at the top of the form, with the address, day and date of the show below it, followed by the entry fee. (Always check to see if Junior Showmanship gets a price break.) *"Entries close"* tells you the date that your entry blank has to be at the superintendent's office. Be sure to mail it in plenty of time. The form also tells what name to make out the check or money order. You must do this properly or your entry will be refused.

The main body of the entry blank is easy to fill in if you take it one step at a time. BREED means the breed of dog you will be taking into the ring. VARIETY (1) is explained under **INSTRUCTIONS** on the back of the form. If the breed you are showing has a variety, you <u>must</u> fill in this blank. (Know your breed!) SEX means the dog's sex, not yours. DOG SHOW CLASS (2) (3) and CLASS DIVISION pertain to conformation classes in which you compete for Championship points or for Best of Breed. You only need to fill in these spaces if you are showing your dog towards its Championship as well as in Junior Handling classes. (These two sections are further explained under **INSTRUCTIONS** on the back of the form.)

ADDITIONAL CLASSES also pertains to conformation classes, as it is possible to show your dog in as many classes as he is eligible. OBEDIENCE TRIAL CLASS is a space used only if you

```
┌─────────────────────────────────────────────────────────┐
│          OFFICIAL AMERICAN KENNEL CLUB ENTRY FORM         │
│                                                           │
│                                                           │
│ I ENCLOSE $ . . . . . . . . .  for entry fees             │
│ IMPORTANT—Read Carefully Instructions on Reverse Side     │
│ Before Filling Out. Numbers in the boxes indicate         │
│ sections of the instructions relevant to the information  │
│ needed in that box (PLEASE PRINT)                         │
│ BREED            VARIETY [1]              SEX             │
│                                                           │
│ DOG [2] [3]                  CLASS [ ]                     │
│ SHOW                         DIVISION                      │
│ CLASS                        Weight color etc              │
│                                                           │
│ ADDITIONAL       OBEDIENCE        JR SHOWMANSHIP          │
│ CLASSES          TRIAL            CLASS                    │
│                  CLASS                                     │
│ NAME OF (See Back)                                        │
│ JUNIOR HANDLER (if any)                                   │
│ FULL                                                      │
│ NAME                                                      │
│ OF DOG                                                     │
│                      Enter number here                    │
│ [ ] AKC REG NO              DATE OF                        │
│ [ ] AKC LITTER NO           BIRTH                         │
│ [ ] ILP NO                                                │
│ [ ] FOREIGN REG NO & COUNTRY  PLACE OF [ ] USA [ ] Canada │
│                               BIRTH              [ ] Foreign│
│ BREEDER                       Do not print the above in catalog│
│                                                           │
│ SIRE                                                      │
│                                                           │
│ DAM                                                       │
│                                                           │
│ ACTUAL OWNER(S) _____                                  │
│ [4]              (Please Print)                            │
│ OWNER'S ADDRESS _____                                   │
│ CITY _____ STATE _____ ZIP _____                       │
│ NAME OF OWNERS AGENT                                      │
│ (IF ANY) AT THE SHOW _____                              │
│ I CERTIFY that I am the actual owner of the dog, or that  │
│ I am the duly authorized agent of the actual owner whose  │
│ name I have entered above. In consideration of the        │
│ acceptance of this entry, I (we) agree to abide by the    │
│ rules and regulations of The American Kennel Club in      │
│ effect at the time of this show or obedience trial, and   │
│ by any additional rules and regulations appearing in the  │
│ premium list for this show or obedience trial or both,    │
│ and further agree to be bound by the "Agreement" printed  │
│ on the reverse side of this entry form. I (we) certify    │
│ and represent that the dog entered is not a hazard to     │
│ persons or other dogs. This entry is submitted for        │
│ acceptance on the foregoing representation and agreement. │
│ SIGNATURE of owner or his agent                           │
│ duly authorized to make this entry _____               │
└─────────────────────────────────────────────────────────┘
```

Official American Kennel Club Entry Form

are showing your dog towards an obedience title or additional obedience honors.

Next is your space: JUNIOR SHOWMANSHIP CLASS. To fill in this space, look in the front of the premium list to see how the show-giving club is dividing the classes. The possibilities might include Novice/Open; Novice Junior/Novice Senior; Open Junior/Open Senior; and Novice Junior Boys/Novice Junior Girls. (The qualifications for each class were outlined in Chapter 1, page 9, "What is Junior Showmanship".) Once you are sure you know the class in which you can compete, list this class in the space provided. NAME OF JUNIOR HANDLER is your name, of course.

FULL NAME OF DOG means the exact name that is on your dog's AKC registration paper. (It is a good idea to keep this registration paper handy, but in a safe place.) Then you must enter his AKC REGISTRATION NUMBER in the space below. Within this section you will also see a box for ILP NUMBER. This is a special type of number which the AKC assigns dogs that do not have an AKC litter registration slip. The AKC assigns a number for the purpose of entering dog shows. This requires a special procedure. If you want to know more about it, contact the AKC. Another box is for FOREIGN REGISTRATION NUMBER. Check this space if your dog was born in another country and imported to the United States. Both the registration number and the name of the country must be indicated.

Check carefully and list his DATE OF BIRTH as shown on the AKC paper. If you do not know your dog's PLACE OF BIRTH, ask your parents to help you find it. BREEDER is also shown on the AKC registration paper, and you must list it exactly as shown on this paper. SIRE and DAM (father and mother) are listed on the paper as well.

Now fill out the box for ACTUAL OWNER(S). Print the name(s) and address carefully. This information is needed so the club can send you a confirmation stating that your entry was received in time, was correct, and that you are entered in the class you requested. Make sure that your dog's owner (if other than yourself) signs the entry form and lists a contact telephone number at the bottom of the form.

The NAME OF OWNER'S AGENT is only completed if a professional handler will be showing the same dog in one of the other classes at this same show.

Now for the back of the entry form. You must fill in the box at the bottom of the form with the required information so that your entry will be complete.

Your JUNIOR HANDLER ID number is obtained from the AKC Events Records Department. To get your number, you must call this department (212-696-8281). Someone will ask you a few questions and then assign you a number. It will only take a few minutes; but be sure to ask your parents for permission to make the call, as it will be a long distance call for most of you.

JUNIOR'S DATE OF BIRTH is your birth date. Then list your ADDRESS, CITY, STATE, and ZIP CODE. Below that information you will find a question pertaining to ownership of your dog. If you are not the owner, then you must tell what relationship you are to the owner, such as son or daughter, etc. If you have any questions about dog ownership, refer to your AKC rule book.

Single copies of the latest editions of the "Rules Applying to Registration and Dog Shows" and "Obedience Regulations" may be obtained WITHOUT CHARGE from any superintendent at shows or from THE AMERICAN KENNEL CLUB, 51 MADISON AVENUE, NEW YORK, N.Y. 10010.

AGREEMENT

I (we) acknowledge that the "Rules Applying to Registration and Dog Shows" and, if this entry is for an Obedience trial, the "Obedience Regulations," have been made available to me (us), and that I am (we are) familiar with their contents. I (we) agree that the club holding this show or obedience trial has the right to refuse this entry for cause which the club shall deem to be sufficient. In consideration of the acceptance of this entry and of the holding of the show or obedience trial and of the opportunity to have the dog judged and to win prize money, ribbons, or trophies, I (we) agree to hold this club, its members, directors, governors, officers, agents, superintendents or show secretary, and any employees of the aforementioned parties, harmless from any claim for loss or injury which may be alleged to have been caused directly or indirectly to any person or thing by the act of this dog while in or upon the show or obedience trial premises or grounds or near any entrance thereto, and I (we) personally assume all responsibility and liability for any such, claim; and I (we) further agree to hold the aforementioned parties harmless from any claim for loss of this dog by disappearance, theft, death or otherwise, and from any claim for damage or injury to the dog, whether such loss, disappearance, theft, damage, or injury, be caused or alleged to be caused by the negligence of the club or any of the parties aforementioned, or by the negligence of any other person, or any other cause or causes.

I (we) hereby assume the sole responsibility for and agree to indemnify and save the aforementioned parties harmless from any and all loss and expense (including legal fees) by reason of the liability imposed by law upon any of the aforementioned parties for damage because of bodily injuries, including death at any time resulting therefrom, sustained by any persons or persons, including myself (ourselves), or on account of damage to property, arising out of or in consequence of my (our) participation in this show or obedience trial, howsoever such injuries, death or damage to property may be caused, and whether or not the same may have been caused or may be alleged to have been caused by negligence of the aforementioned parties or any of their employees or agents, or any other persons.

INSTRUCTIONS

1. (Variety) If you are entering a dog of a breed in which there are varieties for show purposes, please designate the particular variety you are entering, i.e., Cocker Spaniel (Black, ASCOB, parti-color), Beagles (not exceeding 13 in.; over 13 in. but not exceeding 15 in.), Dachshunds (long-haired, smooth, wirehaired), Bull Terriers (colored, white), Manchester Terriers (standard, toy), Chihuahuas (smooth coat, long coat), English Toy Spaniels (King Charles and Ruby, Blenheim and Prince Charles). Poodles (toy, miniature, standard), Collies (rough, smooth).

2. The following categories of dogs may be entered and shown in Best of Breed Competition: Dogs that are Champions of Record and dogs which, according to their owner's records, have completed the requirements for a championship, but whose championships are unconfirmed. The showing of unconfirmed Champions in Best of Breed competition is Limited to a period of 90 days from the date of the show where the dog completed the requirements for a championship.

3. (Dog Show Class) Consult the classification in this premium list. If the dog show class in which you are entering your dog is divided, then, in addition to designating the class, specify the particular division of the class in which you are entering your dog, i.e., age division, color division, weight division.

4. A dog must be entered in the name of the person who actually owned it at the time entries for a show closed. If a registered dog has been acquired by a new owner it must be entered in the name of its new owner in any show for which entries closed after the date of aquirement, regardless of whether the new owner has received the registration certificate indicating that the dog is recorded in his name. State on the entry form whether transfer application has been mailed to A.K.C. (For complete rule refer to Chapter 14, Section 3.)

If this entry is for Jr. Showmanship please give the following information:

JUNIOR SHOWMANSHIP

Jr. Handler ID # _____   JR'S. DATE OF BIRTH _____

ADDRESS _____

CITY_____STATE_____ZIP_____

If Jr. Handler is not the owner of the dog
identified on the face of this form, what is the
relationship of the Jr. Handler to the owner?

Double check your entry form before you send it. Once it is in the mail, it is too late to change anything. Then send your form, along with a check or money order for the entry fee, to the *superintendent* listed on the front of the premium list. Never send cash through the mail. **Also double check the address on the envelope before you send it.**

About a week before the show, you will get a notification back from the superintendent. It indicates your ring time, ring number, arm band number, how to get to the show site, and a few other bits of information. Save this notification, and take it to the show with you. You may find occasion to use it there or beforehand.

Show Day

On the day you are to show, make sure you allow plenty of travel time. Arrive at the show site about an hour before you are scheduled to go into the ring. The schedule you receive back with your entry will tell you the time your class is expected to begin. It may be later, but AKC rules do not allow classes to start earlier than the scheduled time. You will be surprised how fast that hour will speed by as you make your last minute preparations for showing in your class.

If you are handling a coated dog, he will look better if you groom him thoroughly the day before the show. Then, do a second, last-minute grooming just before you go into the ring. Pack all the grooming equipment that you will need the night before your show. You may want to wear a T-shirt and jeans while you groom, and then change into your show clothes at the show. You will also need water and a bowl for your dog, a clean show lead, and possibly your dog's crate and a grooming table.

What To Wear

Appearance is one of the things on which the judge will score you in the ring. You should dress appropriately. Cut-offs jeans, sweats and T-shirts are out! The judge cannot rate you on your clothes, but rather on whether you have made an effort to look as if you want to win and are neat and clean.

Plan what you are going to wear ahead of time. Choose clothes that are neat, but comfortable. Never dress in your fanciest outfit—you'll probably feel uncomfortable and that will keep you from showing your dog to the best advantage. Choose an outfit that looks good with your breed of dog, in colors that contrast with the dog's coat color so the dog will stand out. You and your dog want to make a nice picture when seen together in the ring.

Wear comfortable shoes that allow you to run easily. Rubber or crepe soled shoes will help your footing on the show mats used in indoor show rings and on the grass in outdoor show rings.

A sport coat and tie or dress shirt and pants are appropriate for boys. A dress, blouse with matching skirt of appropriate length, or a pantsuit is appropriate for girls. Your appearance will tell the judge whether you take your sport seriously.

THE SHOW SITE

Every show site will have certain places set aside for exercising your dog. Walk around a little bit, getting your dog used to the sounds and smells and excitement of the show. As you're walking, keep an eye out for your ring. Walk over to the ring and take a look at the size, shape, and physical conditions of the area. Note if it is an indoor or outdoor ring, and whether there are any dips, holes, or other unusual conditions to look out for when you are finally in the ring. If you are showing in an indoor ring, check to see that the mats are lying flat. You don't want to trip over an upturned edge.

Walk over to the steward's table, placed just inside the entrance to your ring, to see if you can pick up your arm band yet. Also, if you have any last minute grooming to do, it's best to do it while you still have a few minutes to spare.

AT RINGSIDE

About ten minutes before your scheduled time to go into the ring, put on your arm band and take your dog to ringside. The judges at a dog show are <u>not</u> required to wait for exhibitors, so don't be late! However, they will <u>never</u> start before the scheduled time. The larger dogs (and their exhibitors) usually go to the front of the line because they are able to move faster than the smaller dogs. If the judge wants you lined up in any other way, the ring steward will let you know as you enter the ring. Once you are in the ring, the judge will give you other instructions.

WHAT WILL THE JUDGE LOOK FOR?

The judge will evaluate you and the other handlers in four basic things.

1. You are to present your dog in the right way for the breed you are handling. In 4-H classes where you can show a mixed-breed dog, you should handle your dog as you would the breed he most resembles. The judge will watch to see if you know how to move and stack your dog just as that breed is in regular breed (conformation) classes at a dog show.

2. The judge will rate you on whether you "over" or "under" handle your dog or whether you correctly present your dog in a quiet, easy manner. You should not draw attention to yourself or your handling. The judge is looking for the junior with a natural "hand for dogs." You will lose points if you block or distract the judge's vision of the dog.

3. You must know the various ring patterns and be able to follow the judge's directions. The judge will watch for handlers that are alert and prepared for a change in the routine.

4. Another factor the judge considers is your appearance and behavior. That means you should be confident and business-like, taking the class seriously. As mentioned above, you will be rated on your neatness and whether you are dressed appropriately. Finally, the judge will look for the junior who is polite, who does not crowd or disturb the other dogs, and who is kind and alert to the needs of his dog.

Good Sportsmanship

Good sportsmanship in Junior Showmanship is one of the most important life lessons you will learn. It is hard for everyone to lose, but it takes a big person to admit losing fairly. There are many shows, and each one has a different set of winners and losers.

Learning how to lose gracefully and how to handle disap-
pointment will come in handy in your adult life. Believe it or not,
adults don't win at everything <u>they</u> try either; we all must learn to
lose. A good sportsman is someone who plays fair and does not
complain when he loses nor brag when he wins. If you can master
this task, you'll be successful in Junior Showmanship, as well as in
life.

Whether you win or lose, always do it gracefully. Like training, this also takes practice! A truly good sport will congratulate
the winners on his way out of the ring. A truly good winner will
encourage the losers and not be too boastful.

Last Minute Reminders

Before your class is called, take a few last minutes to
review these points that will help you make a winning performance.

SMILE

It's important to smile in the ring, even if you have to force
it at first. You might be so nervous on show day that you'll find it
hard to smile, which is why you need to practice smiling at home,
as part of your training routine. Eventually, it will become natural
for you to smile in the ring. If you aren't smiling in the ring, you're
probably not having fun; and having fun is part of Junior
Showmanship. Judges like to see Handlers and their dogs having
fun together.

NEVER GET BETWEEN YOUR DOG AND THE JUDGE

In addition to smiling, always keep your dog in full view of
the judge; never obstruct the judge's view by coming between
them. Sometimes this can be tricky, but it is an important factor.
The judge is looking to see if you are making your dog "stand out
as the most important part of the team effort," according to the
AKC rule book.

KEEP YOUR EYES ON THE JUDGE AT ALL TIMES

When you enter the Junior Showmanship ring, you and
your dog are to follow every instruction the judge issues. To test
your experience, some judges will use hand signals instead of

words. They are trying to enforce the importance of keeping your eyes on the judge.

The judge will indicate, either with words or signals, when he wants you to gait your dog or stop, <u>where</u> he wants you to stop, and in what specific pattern he wants you to move your dog dur-ing the individual examination. To prevent making an error, keep looking at the judge to see what he is doing, where he is standing, and how soon he may want you to do something specific. Being on your toes and ready to respond to his slightest command will impress any judge.

If the judge is busy examining another dog and handler farther down the line, he will not expect you to keep your dog stacked in the show stance during this time. You may use this time to let your dog relax unless the judge is constantly looking back at the line each time he examines a dog. Just keep your eyes on the judge! When your turn is approaching, get back to business with your dog. Don't get caught unaware.

Your dog will work better and have more energy if you don't demand that he stay stacked continually. However, this does not mean that you can lean against the nearest post and fall asleep. Keep talking to your dog so that you always have his attention. DON'T talk to friends and relatives outside the ring. The judge could glance around the ring at any time, and he should always find you working with your dog. Talking to your dog and patting him falls into the work category, which is one of several performance categories.

Keep your eye out for the last dog to be examined; when that dog is performing his gait, be ready to set your dog in a show stance again. The judge will then step into the middle of the ring and will expect to see every dog stacked properly. Keep all your attention centered on your dog, the judge, and the handlers directly in front of and behind you. This concentrated effort will be obvious to the judge. Your dog will also realize that you have your eye on him and will not try to misbehave.

Chapter 6

Techniques And Patterns In The Ring

You will enter the ring circling in a counter clockwise direction. The judge may move all the dogs and handlers around the ring several times before examining the dogs individually, or he may examine the dogs individually and then gait them all together. While you are gaiting your dog, the judge will watch to see if your dog responds well to you and if you appear to work as a team. You should have your dog under control and moving smoothly at a trot at all times, without getting in the way of the other dogs and handlers.

Controlling Your Dog

While you are in the ring, it is most important that you have complete control of your dog at all times. Dogs get loose; and if this happens to you, go get your dog and return to your position quickly. To prevent your dog from even trying to get away, communicate with him. Keep just enough tension on the lead that he knows you're paying attention to his actions. Talking quietly to him will also help keep his mind on you and off mischief.

One more word about control. It does <u>not</u> mean yanking your dog around. Control is a firm, steady hand on the lead and on your dog, guiding him into position. If you are required to move quickly from one place to another, get your dog's attention before you start to move. A pat under the chin or a light jerk-release motion on the lead should be sufficient. The judge does not expect miracles and will be happier with a smooth response to his instructions than with an impatient jerk. You will also get more cooperation from your dog when you are not jerking him around senselessly.

Stacking Your Dog

As you stack your dog whenever you notice the judge looking, remember that he is looking at the picture the two of you make as a team. He is also checking to see if you can control your dog, and if you know how to minimize your dog's major faults. He looks for a team that is relaxed and looks as if they want to win. Also, he wants to see your dog looking interested and responding to you.

When you are presenting your dog for his physical examination, you must keep control over his whole body. Stroking him
slowly and gently on the belly is soothing and will keep him from
getting excited and moving out of place.

As the judge moves toward your dog's rear quarters, you
move to his front quarters to stay out of the way. You may want to
take hold of your dog's muzzle in one or both of your hands. Some
dogs do not like having their rear quarters examined, and even a
well-trained dog can be spooked once in a while. A hand around
your dog's muzzle will help maintain control.

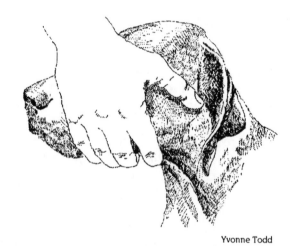

Yvonne Todd

WORKING WITH LARGE BREEDS

If you have a larger breed, it will be to your advantage to
be at ringside early enough to take your dog into the ring first, or
nearly first. Try to group yourself with other dogs (and handlers)
that will be moving at your dog's same pace.

As you move around the ring during the group gait, be
alert; you will probably overtake the small dogs (and their handlers) at the end of the line. Rather than run up too close on a
small dog's hindquarters, slow your pace down in enough time to
avoid such a collision. This will also prevent you from having to
jerk to an awkward halt. If you keep this in mind when you start
your gait, you will turn in a much smoother performance.

When stacking your large dog for the judge, you may want to kneel on one knee (preferably the left knee) and leave your right foot on the ground. This position allows you to be close to your dog so that you can comfort him, if needed. It is easy to get up quickly from this position, so you won't have a problem moving your dog at a moment's notice.

Keep an eye out as you stack your larger dog in case a handler with a small dog has come up behind you. Sometimes you will be concentrating so hard on stacking your own dog that you may come close to stepping on a small dog behind you. Develop what is called *ring awareness*, or the ability to see or sense where others in the ring are and what they are doing.

WORKING WITH SMALL DOGS

Small dogs have a dainty appearance and you should show them in a graceful style suitable to this appearance. When stacking them on the ground, kneel down or even sit back on your heels to work with them. Be careful not to hover over small dogs, as your body can easily hide them. Keep the lead folded in your hand if you have no grooming to do in the ring. If you have a long-haired small breed that requires constant touchups, flip the lead around your neck. This will leave both hands free for grooming and still keep it out of the way.

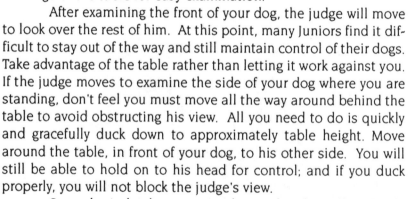

Most small dogs stand on a table during their physical examinations. This calls for much practice at home so your dog will feel comfortable working high off the ground.

In the ring, carry your dog over to the table when the judge motions for your turn. Stack him so that the length of his body is parallel to the length of the table and his head is close to the edge of the table for easy examination.

After examining the front of your dog, the judge will move to look over the rest of him. At this point, many Juniors find it difficult to stay out of the way and still maintain control of their dogs. Take advantage of the table rather than letting it work against you. If the judge moves to examine the side of your dog where you are standing, don't feel you must move all the way around behind the table to avoid obstructing his view. All you need to do is quickly and gracefully duck down to approximately table height. Move around the table, in front of your dog, to his other side. You will still be able to hold on to his head for control; and if you duck properly, you will not block the judge's view.

Once the judge has examined your dog, he will probably ask you to gait your dog for him. Being careful where you place your body in relation to the judge, lift your small dog down to the ground and take the time to get your lead straightened out. By now, you will know what pattern to follow. Then you can make your courtesy turn and begin to gait your dog.

Once in a while you will find yourself in a ring without an examination table. The judge will have to examine your small dog while he is stacked on the ground. This can sometimes unsettle a dog that has become used to meeting judges at eye level. To have a stranger looming above may spook your small dog, so practice stacking him for his physical examination both ways to be prepared for any circumstance.

Showing The Bite

Junior Showmanship is different from conformation class-es because you need to develop a wider variety of handling tech-niques. One such technique is "*showing the bite.*"

Showing the bite requires <u>you</u> to show the judge your dog's bite. This does not mean opening your dog's mouth and showing off his tonsils! The judge wants to examine your dog's teeth.

Many breed standards are specific about how your dog's teeth should meet. The judge needs to determine whether your dog's teeth fit the breed standard; and he needs a clear view to do so.

To show the bite, transfer the lead to your right hand (keeping it folded up neatly). Grasp your dog's lower jaw with your right hand, with your thumb underneath the loose skin at the tip of his mouth. Your left hand should come over the top of your dog's muzzle and gently grasp his lips with your left thumb. Then carefully pull his lips apart. This gives a clear view of your dog's bite and causes the least amount of discomfort for him.

Practice showing the bite every day, several times a day. The more you practice, the more nonchalant your dog will become about subjecting himself to this indignity. You should both be

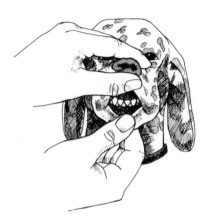

comfortable about doing this before you go into the ring for the first time. Never try anything for the first time when you are in competition—always take time to practice at home first.

Showing The Off Side

Once the judge has examined your dog's bite, he will proceed to examine the rest of your dog. During this further examination, you will need to be able to work from both sides of your dog. The most common position to show your dog is from his left (or show) side while you work from his right (or off) side. However, sometimes the judge will want to view the right side of your dog, and you will have to feel at ease working from his left side. This technique is called *showing the off side*.

You will also have to develop the skill of changing sides while keeping your dog under control. The way you move from one side of your dog to the other will depend upon the direction from which the judge approaches you. If the judge comes towards you from the front of your dog, you must change sides by going around your dog's rear end.

If the judge comes toward you from the back of your dog, you must change sides by going around your dog's head. NEVER step over your dog's back! Changing to the off side is a difficult maneuver, and it takes practice to do this gracefully. This is an impressive move when done correctly. It could get you that first-place ribbon if you demonstrate to the judge that you have taken the time to learn how to do this move.

Keep in mind this cardinal rule when showing the off side: <u>Never come between the judge and your dog!</u> It will take practice, but eventually you will be able to keep your dog alert and immobile in a show stance while both you and the judge move around his body.

While the judge is examining your dog's head, stay by your dog's rear end. As the judge moves down your dog's body, you must move to the front of your dog to get out of the way. Some judges, to test how alert you are, will continue to move on around your dog to view his right, or off, side. Because this is the side you normally work from, if you now return to this position, you will come between the judge and your dog. You must, therefore, take up a position on the opposite side—or show side—from which you normally work! If you have not practiced this maneuver with your dog at home, he will probably react by breaking his show stance. Don't be caught off guard. Surprise your dog at home so that he will not be surprised in the ring later.

The Courtesy Turn

Once the judge has examined your dog (and examined your skill at keeping out of his way), he will ask you to move your dog in a specific pattern. PAY ATTENTION to what he tells you! Never assume that he will ask you to move in the same pattern as he asked the handler before you to move. To test your attentiveness, he may ask you to move in an entirely different pattern. There is no substitute for paying attention.

Gather the lead up in your left hand so that nothing remains dangling. It is distracting, to both the judge and your dog, to have the tail end of a show lead bouncing around as you move.

Walk to the place the judge indicated he wished you to start your movement pattern. Then, before starting into a show gait with your dog, make a *courtesy turn* in front of the judge.

The courtesy turn is simply a semicircle movement executed directly in front of the judge. It gives him one final look at you and your dog before you both start your gait away from him. The courtesy turn will also ease your dog into a smooth start for his proper show gait.

To execute a correct courtesy turn, keep your dog on your left side and move to a position directly in front of the judge.

Then, keeping your body in one place, guide your dog in a semi-circle around you so that your dog passes between you and the judge. As your dog is completing this semicircle, be prepared to guide him into a show gait on a path leading directly away from the judge.

The use of the courtesy turn indicates to the judge that you are trying for a more polished handling technique. The better you can execute the turn, the better you can show your handling abil-ity. Ideally, you should use the courtesy turn in all instances when the judge asks you to move your dog.

Gaiting Patterns Used In The Ring

The "O" Pattern

The "O" or *circle pattern* has two different uses. The most common use of the pattern is when the judge has everyone move around the ring together. In this instance, he is testing each handler's control of his own dog and his ability to react to unusual circumstances. He will watch to see how you pace your dog between the handler and dog in front of and behind you. He wants to know how you react if your dog is slower or faster than the others. He will see whether you keep an eye on the handler in front of you, in case he stops suddenly.

Occasionally, a judge will ask you to move your dog in a circle by yourself. This is one time when the courtesy turn may be too awkward to use. If the judge is standing in front of your dog or on his off side, you may be able to gracefully execute a courtesy turn before running the circle. If the judge is standing near the center of the ring, a courtesy turn would be out of place. Using the courtesy turn in the "O" pattern is a matter of judgment. Do what makes you feel most comfortable.

As you move in the circle shape, keep one eye on the judge so that you can finish your circle by stopping gracefully in front of him. Learn to gauge your dog's speed so that you know how fast he will cover the ground between you and the judge. Then you won't suddenly bump into the judge.

A judge may surprise you with a variation of the "O" pattern. He may use this when there are many good handlers in the ring, and he's trying to pick out the best ones. Don't let this variation catch you off guard. What he will do is ask everyone to move their dogs around the ring two or three times. Then, when you're not watching, he will quickly move from the center to one side of the ring. If you haven't kept your eye on him, you will suddenly find yourself doing your gait between your dog and the judge.

To avoid this dilemma, keep one eye on the judge and one eye on your dog. When you see the judge move, be prepared to switch to the show side of your dog. To do this gracefully, allow your dog to get slightly ahead of you; and, as you continue running, pass behind him to his show side. As you are passing behind him, switch the lead from your left hand to your right hand. Once you have passed the judge, follow the same procedure to get back to your dog's off side.

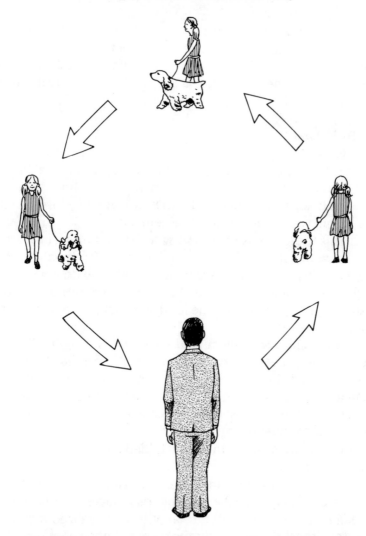

Another way to get back to your dog's off side smoothly is to execute a semicircle in front of him. Lead with your left foot and turn away from him to get back to your normal position. These are both tricky maneuvers that look good when you have practiced and can execute them correctly. Taking the time to perfect the "O" pattern could make a big difference someday.

The "L" Pattern

Now, let's assume that the judge asked you to move your dog in an "L" *pattern*. The pattern looks like the capital letter L, if

viewed from above. To do this move, walk in a straight line away
from the judge, who is standing at the top of the L shape. As you
come to the corner of the L shape, make a sharp left turn and continue walking to the end of the L shape. Then turn and retrace
your steps exactly.

Lead Switching

Now, close your eyes for a minute and imagine you are in
the ring with your dog doing the "L" pattern. To avoid breaking the
cardinal rule of Junior Showmanship, you must find a way to
change your dog to your right side. That will put him closest to the
judge before you retrace your "L" pattern steps.

This technique is called *lead switching*; and with a little practice, you will soon be able to do it like a professional handler.
Make the switch quickly and accurately so that you do not confuse
your dog or throw him off stride. Maintaining control of your dog
and keeping a secure hold on the leash are your principal concerns
in learning this technique.

A helpful way to learn lead switching is to watch it being
done in the ring. Lead switching is a difficult technique to master.
You must switch the lead from one hand to another while also
retaining control of your dog as you maneuver him in a change of
direction. All the judge should notice is a directed pattern executed with great finesse and smoothness.

For starters, keep the lead folded neatly in your hand.
Lead switching will be much easier to learn if you have first
learned to control the lead in your hand. Think of lead switching
as the baton hand-off in the Olympic relay races. You have seen
one teammate hand the baton to another and realized that if the
baton was dropped it would put the team out of competition. You
will be transferring the lead from one hand to the other, not to a
second party, but the maneuver is nearly as important.

Remember to keep your lead firmly wrapped in the palm of
your hand. You will lose control during switching if the lead unrav-
els when you switch hands. Work on controlling the lead in the
palm of either of your hands. Practice holding it correctly before
you place it on the dog.

As you approach the end of the mat before you turn to
retrace your "L" pattern, extend your left arm and the lead as far as
you can from the side of your body. Begin to guide your dog into

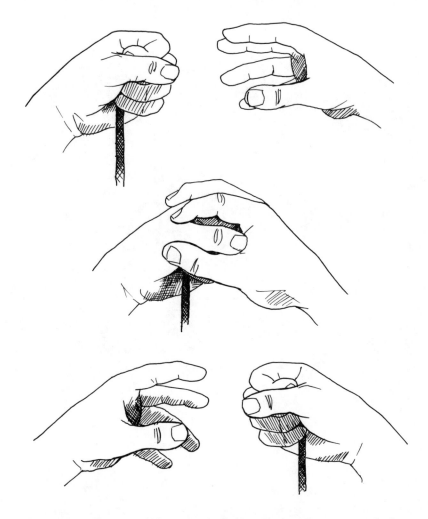

a turn <u>towards</u> you while you are beginning to turn towards him. Then extend your right arm to meet your left arm and grab firmly onto the lead with your right hand, making sure that you have a secure hold on the lead. Now guide your dog into position to start the return trip; he will now be on your right side, and the lead will be in your right hand.

Always leave the judge with your dog on your left side and return with him the same way. This is correct in most gaiting patterns used in the show ring. Once you switch leads at the bottom of the "L" pattern, you must switch leads again at the corner of the "L" pattern. This puts your dog back on your left side as you return to the judge.

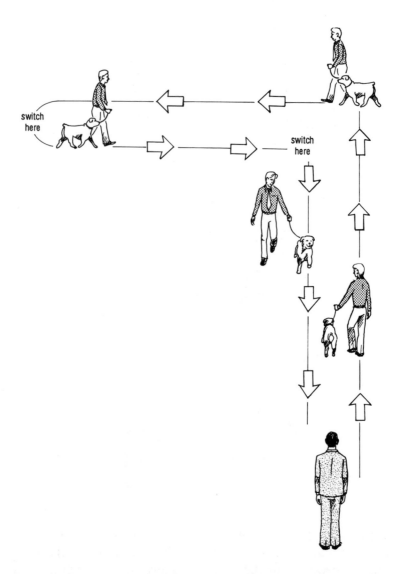

Think of the lead like a steering wheel, and practice switching the lead as you work your dog on different patterns. Only practice will achieve that perfect teamwork that will make you winners.

Many judges will automatically start walking around your
dog after you bring him to a halt in front of them. It seems that
the majority of judges instinctively head for the show side, or left
side, of your dog to view his profile as you stop him. If you do not
switch hands at the corner of the "L" pattern, you allow your dog

to remain on your right side. This hides his show side from the judge's view.

You switch leads at the corner of the "L" exactly as done at the bottom of the "L," except in reverse. Always remember to keep a tight hold on the lead and to guide your dog through the turn. Again, this is a tricky maneuver. Practice at home before you try it in the ring.

Once in a while, because of the way the ring has been set up, a judge may ask you to move your dog in a reverse "L" pattern. You will again start at the top of the L-shape and follow the same path to the corner, with your dog on your left side. However, when you reach the corner, you must lead-switch there when you make the turn to the right so that your dog ends up on your right side. Guide your dog into a half circle turn towards you in which he moves out and away from you while you make a half circle turn in the opposite direction. Then switch your lead as you both make a quarter turn to the left and proceed down the bottom leg of the "L." Your dog should now be on your right side. On the return trip, perform a lead switch at the bottom of the "L," so your dog is again on your left side. Turn the corner of the "L" and return home with your dog remaining on your left side.

THE TRIANGLE PATTERN

The *triangle pattern* looks like a triangle, if viewed from above. If the judge indicates that he wants you to move your dog in a triangle pattern, start by making the courtesy turn in front of him. Then move your dog down the same path as you did for the L pattern. When you come to the end of the L, do not retrace your steps. Instead, turn towards the judge and walk at an angle back to the top of the L shape, forming a triangle.

The triangle pattern is easy because you do not have to switch leads. The only thing that you should do is make another

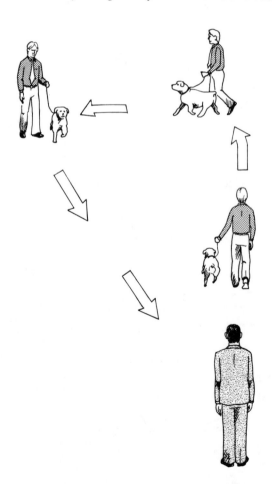

courtesy turn at the bottom of the L shape before you start walking back to the judge. This gets your dog moving in the right stride
and you won't put your knee into his side when you turn to walk
back. This looks a lot cleaner than guiding your dog through the
turn with your lead.

The triangle pattern is the simplest pattern of all in which
to perform. You are never between your dog and the judge. You
return to the judge with your dog on your left side, just as when
you started, and you don't have to switch leads. Some Juniors
even feel that the courtesy turn in the corner is not a necessary
move. If you wish, you can leave it out until you feel more at ease
in the ring. However, the courtesy turn gives you time to glance up
and see where the judge is standing. Sometimes you will be showing outdoors, with no mats to follow, and you will have to spot his
location so that you can head directly towards him. There is nothing more embarrassing than heading back to the general direction
of the judge and then finding him fifteen feet away from where you
stopped! Some Juniors, because they do not see the judge before
finishing the third leg of the triangle, end up running a "U" pattern,
which is not exactly what the judge ordered. Just keep your wits
about you, and you'll do fine.

THE "T" PATTERN

The "T" *pattern* is the most difficult of all the patterns to
master because you must do a great deal of lead-switching, and
your dog will be changing gaits and directions frequently. If properly done, this move gives you a chance to show off your skills.

The "T" is the traditional pattern used in the group rings of
conformation competition, so you can get your practice in there,
as well as at home. Then, when you and your dog begin Junior
Showmanship, you will turn in a smooth performance for the
judge! If the judge asks you to move your dog in a "T" pattern, he
will most likely be standing at the bottom of the "T." Begin by
moving your dog in the usual courtesy turn. Start moving up the
stem of the "T" towards the top. When you reach the top of the "T,"
guide your dog into a left turn and move along the left half of the
top of the "T." When you reach the end of the left half, make a lead-
switch exactly as you would for the "L" pattern. Then, turn and
come back along the top of the "T." Don't stop in the middle.
Continue all the way to the other side of the top of the "T."

At this point, execute another lead-switch (in reverse of the one you just did on the other side of the top). If you have been following these steps in your imagination so far, you will now realize that the lead is back in your left hand, with your dog on your left side.

Now move halfway across the top of the "T" back to where you started your cross pattern. Spot where the judge is standing, and head back towards him. If you choose, you can execute another courtesy turn at the top before starting down the stem. As mentioned before, the addition of the courtesy turn will help you get your dog under control for that last run towards the judge. It will also give you time to look up and see where the judge is standing.

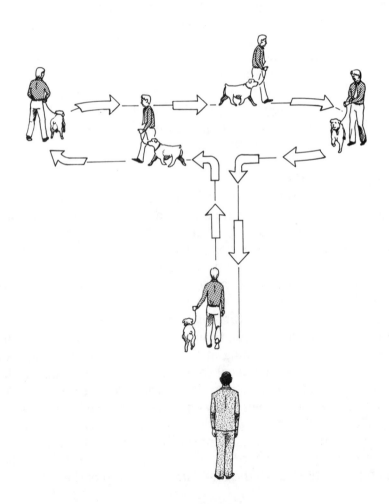

THE "I" PATTERN

The judge might say to you, "Take your dog straight down and back, please." This is also referred to as the "I" *pattern,* although the judge won't call it by that name.

His request sounds simple, but don't get caught with your guard down. Many Juniors forget to do the courtesy turn because "straight down and back" sounds so easy. <u>Always</u> start with a courtesy turn; then move your dog away from the judge on the path he indicates—with your dog on your left side, as usual. At the end of your run, pivot around in a half circle to your right. Pause to get your dog under control, and then glance up to see where the judge is standing. A clever judge, who is having a hard time choosing between good handlers, might try to pull a fast one on you. As you move your dog straight down, he may step five feet to one side.

If you fail to glance up and locate the judge before your return, you can be caught off guard. You may stop in front of where the judge WAS instead of where he IS. There is no graceful way to recover from this error, so try your best to avoid making it. One other hint may keep you in the ribbons: Don't pivot to the left when you reach the end of your straight down run. Your dog will not be expecting you to turn towards him, and you may inadvertently give him a knee in the side. Or, in the case of a small dog, you might trip over him.

Some Juniors execute a lead-switch at the end of the straight down run as they turn to come back to the judge. This is not necessary, but if you use the lead-switch, remember that you will be working from the dog's right side when you stop in front of the judge. This calls for at-home practice so you feel comfortable working your dog from either side.

Moving Two Dogs Together

Once in a while, the judge may point to you and one other Junior and ask the two of you to move your dogs straight down and back together. He will be judging your ability to keep your dog under control when in proximity to another dog, as well as your ability to pace yourself to another handler's gait.

When using this technique, both handlers move in the "I" pattern with their dogs walking on the inside. They will each have to execute a lead change at the top of the "I" so that the dogs remain together on the inside and the handlers remain on the outside.

Then turn your dog <u>towards you</u> rather than towards the other dog. This will prevent the two dogs from making eye contact with each other and keep them out of mischief.

When performing this technique, you must be extremely alert as you gait your dog because many dogs are unable to resist the temptation to play. Maintaining lead tension and speaking softly to your dog will let him know that you are watching his every move and that he must pay no attention to the other dog.

A really clever judge will pick out a small dog and a large dog to gait together. There will be a marked difference in their gaits, and it is a challenge to you as a handler to keep your dog moving smoothly and in <u>unison</u>. The handler of the smaller dog should set the pace. The handler of the larger dog may even have to move him at a walking pace to keep the two dogs together. The slower you move a dog, the harder you have to work to keep his attention. If you stay alert, you will do just fine.

Because you need another handler and dog, it is a little harder to practice this movement. Perhaps you can get together with another Junior to practice this drill. The fewer surprises you can spring on your dog in the ring, the better.

What The Judge Looks For 🐕

We have been discussing the need for teamwork between you and your dog, but there are other things that a judge will look for, both positive and negative. Some things you may not have thought about can ruin your chances for winning.

It is important that you do not develop what I call "theatrics" in the ring. Several handling techniques that fall into this category come to mind. One is the handler who stands two feet away from the dog with the lead extended to its fullest extent. Don't get carried away with fads—use proper presentation for your breed. I cannot stress enough the importance of maintaining control of your dog. If you use this stance and someone drops a chair outside the ring, what will happen? You could easily lose your dog because he spooks from the noise and bolts from the ring.

Another theatrical move is called the "chicken wing"—when a handler places her free hand on or behind her hip bone as she gaits the dog. It is unlikely that you would put your hands on your hips if you were running a race at school. It looks unnatural in the show ring, too. A judge will look for correct and natural movement. Unnatural moves and gestures distract the judge.

Something else that is very noticeable to a judge as soon as he or she walks into the ring is what we commonly refer to as "the mechanical dog." This happens when you have simply overtrained your dog and the dog performs before he is asked. This is often apparent when you do one of the gaiting patterns. The dog will start making turns or changing sides without his handler's guidance. Or, the dog may set himself up for the presentation and stand still through the entire class without any direction from you.

Remember, it is important that your dog be well trained before you begin to show. It is equally important that the dog works in such a way as to show off your handling skills, not do it all by himself. Judges want to see you work at presenting your dog to them, so be careful that your dog doesn't know the routine so well that he does everything without you.

You and your dog should both appear to be relaxed and enjoying the class. If you are nervous, the dog will often pick up your tension through the lead and begin to feel nervous, too. He may shy away from the judge, or not let the judge touch him at all. Showing should be fun, and the judge will look for a dog and handler team that looks as if they are enjoying themselves. Your dog will work better and have more energy if you don't demand that he stay stacked continually.

RING WORK

Talking to your dog and patting him is very important and is one of several work categories that you will be scored on. Other work categories depend on the individual judge. Some judges expect you to have your dog stacked and standing at attention each time they have finished examining a competitor and turn back to look at the line-up. Other judges use this when the competition is so tough that they must eliminate some. Any slip on your part looking around outside the ring, not having your dog at attention, can eliminate you from the competition. In such instances it is very important to give your dog a break from stacking when the judge is not looking.

Another work category for the handlers of coated breeds is attention to your dog's grooming. You can carry a brush or comb in the ring. Two widely used placements for carrying them are secured under a belt at the small of your back, or under the rubber band on your arm. Be careful that the brush or comb will not fall out while you are gaiting. Brush or comb your dog's coat back in place after stacking your dog but before the judge comes over to examine him individually.

Of course, if your dog is short coated there is not much you can do compared to your fellow handlers exhibiting coated breeds.

Always watch the judge. Watch her eyes to see what part of your dog she is focused on. When you are in a stacked position, always have that part of your dog ready. Set up your dog's left front, then his left rear. This way you will have the show side set up first for the judge. Then do the off or inside front and rear.

If the judge is looking for expression, be sure your dog is looking straight ahead and is alert. If the judge is looking at how you present the head, do it in such a way that the judge feels you have personalized her request. Take hold of the back of your dog's skull and lift up his chin to show the judge what a beautiful head and muzzle your dog has. You may hold the lead either in one hand or dropped to the side of the dog's shoulders, but gather it up quickly after inspection.

You will never be caught off guard if you remember to watch the judge's eyes and movements. The judge might ask you to present the dog's front. Here you would set up your dog's front immediately and then set up the rear, or vice versa if he asked to see the rear first. The judge may kneel down at eye level with your dog's topline. It is important that you have your dog stacked properly, not standing high in the rear nor too stretched out. Lean out so you can see what the judge is seeing, and if it does not look right, reset your dog quickly.

If the competition is stiff, the judge may use another tactic. She may purposely move one of your dog's feet. If you are watching the judge, you will pick this up immediately. Now you must decide. Did she move the foot to the correct position as a way of pointing out to you the misplacement? Or, was the placement correct and should you now reset the foot in the same position as it was before? Don't lose confidence in a situation like this. If the foot was correctly placed, move it back to its previous position and reset the opposite foot if necessary. This is what the judge wants to see from you.

Each movement you make in setting up your dog should be quick, easy, and precise. When the class is very competitive, judges have no choice but to test the limits of your handling abilities. If you start to second guess yourself and begin to feel that you made a mistake, the judge will have accomplished the purpose of the test—to bring out any weaknesses.

If, on the other hand, the judge correctly sets your dog's foot, then quickly observe the other three feet to see if they are properly placed. Don't let this frustrate you. NEVER STOP SHOWING until that fourth place position has been chosen, even if you have made a mistake.

The more you perfect your ability to keep your eye on the judge, the better edge you will have on your competition. Recognize that you are being judged on your ability to show your dog the same way as in the breed or conformation ring. You want to make your dog stand out, but never use techniques that are unbecoming to you.

Some "tricks of the trade" used in the Junior Handling ring have no business being there at all. You may see someone upstaging someone else by moving his dog out towards the center of the ring and stacking him to hide the other dogs and handlers down the line. Or someone may purposely run up on you as you are gaiting, allowing his dog to practically step on your dog's heels and bothering you and your dog. Or, worst of all, he may bump into or step on your dog, causing your dog to lose his ability to perform well for you that day.

Junior Handling should consist of turning in a good, smooth, polished performance. If the quality of your handling is consistently good from the time you walk into the ring until the time you leave, you will not need tricks. It is always evident to the judge and to spectators at ringside when a handler has put in time at home working with his dog, training him for competition. Training, not tricking, is the key to winning ribbons in Junior Showmanship.

One <u>good</u> trick, and a perfectly legal one, too, is to wear a smile, in and out of the ring. Make it as genuinely big and happy as possible. A smile gives a finishing touch to your performance and gives you the look of a winner. It doesn't cost a thing and should come naturally to every Junior Handler. If you love exhibiting, the smile will be there, and the ribbons will soon follow. Don't be afraid to look the judge right in the eyes when you smile. Eye contact is a sign of confidence in yourself, your ability, and your performance. Look him right in the eyes and let him know you are proud of what you are doing.

Get A Coach

Being able to identify your own handling faults is often a hard thing to do. If you are having trouble with this, perhaps you could work with a coach to improve your skills.

A coach does not necessarily have to be someone who has been a Junior Handler. Your coach could be a parent or someone involved with dogs in some other way. If having a coach isn't possible for you, a large mirror can be an invaluable guide.

There are many bad habits that you can pick up if you don't (or someone else doesn't) watch out for them. Some important things to watch for include bracing your elbow on your knee while holding up your dog's head, using your dog's back to help you rise from your kneeling position, and baiting improperly.

If you bait your dog, make sure it does not look as if you are just feeding a hungry dog; this is not the purpose of baiting your dog. You are trying to get and keep his attention; just make sure you bait discreetly, trying not to get the attention of the entire line of dogs and handlers behind you.

Remember that Junior Showmanship is communication between you and your dog. Work slow and easy on this communication. A good Junior Handler draws attention to himself because of his ability to interact gracefully and skillfully with his dog in the ring.

Drawing by Yvonne Todd

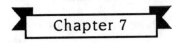

Chapter 7

Beyond Junior Showmanship

Where Do We Go From Here?

Perhaps the most challenging and exciting aspect of Junior Showmanship is that it doesn't have to end with winning a ribbon or two at your local shows, or even with achieving recognition as Best Junior Handler of the Year. Rather, it is often just the beginning of a host of marvelous experiences for the young dog fancier.

As mentioned earlier, you can always have a goal of qualifying for the Westminster Kennel Club finals held in New York City in early February. You can go even further than that, however.

THE WORLD SERIES OF JUNIOR SHOWMANSHIP

The World Series of Junior Showmanship is a series of Junior Showmanship classes held at selected dog shows across the United States each year. The winners of each series will then compete against each other in a final show. The top award winner from this show will have the opportunity to represent the United States in the World Junior Showmanship Competition held each year at the Crufts Dog Show in England.

Unlike the Westminster Finals, which requires eight first-place wins in open competition to enter, there are no special requirements for entering this series. It is also open to both Novice and Open competitors. The winner chosen as the Best Junior Handler at each show in the series will be eligible to compete in the designated finals.

The World Series of Junior Showmanship is sponsored by Kal Kan Pedigree dog food company and is produced by the California-based Newport Dog Shows. The individual shows are held at different locations throughout the United States, giving all Juniors a chance to compete to participate in the finals.

The winner of each series will receive an expense-paid trip for himself and a chaperone to attend the world finals in England. Unlike the requirements of most Junior Handling classes, the World Series finalists also are tested on their knowledge of dogs in three fifteen-minute interviews.

Like any national or international competition, the World Series of Junior Showmanship provides a memorable experience with opportunity to meet other Junior finalists from across the United States.

In addition to the trip to England, the winners of the finals have been awarded a personal computer and a scholarship. The second- and third-place finalists have also received scholarships. The series is highly rated as a notable opportunity to compete against the best Junior Handlers in the world.

Former President Bush commended the World Series of Junior Showmanship as an outstanding credit to Junior Handlers. With the continued sponsorship from Kal Kan Pedigree and guidance from Newport Dog Shows, this series will continue to grow. It encourages young handlers everywhere to keep improving their skills and fostering their love of dogs.

Opportunities Outside The Ring

Young adults have a place in the world of dogs that is above and beyond the limits of the Junior Showmanship ring. After all the time you have spent training, many of you will choose to continue using and expanding the knowledge you've gained.

Most young adults feel that they are as intelligent as their parents, and they're right! The problems that arise between youths and adults are usually due to a lack of communication. Young adults are not always as diplomatic as they could be when expressing their ideas to adults. Adults are not always as receptive as <u>they</u> could be to the ideas of youth. Young people who learn to present their viewpoints diplomatically can have influence in the dog world. Junior Showmanship may just be the beginning of many pleasurable and profitable activities for you.

Following are a few ideas to get you thinking about how you can get further involved in the world of dogs.

BECOME ACTIVE WITH A LOCAL KENNEL CLUB

A good way to spark interest in and support for Junior Handling classes is to become active with a local kennel club. Invite other young people in your area to become involved with you. Young people have boundless energy that can be productively channeled into most clubs; your fresh and original ideas will be beneficial. For example, you could be especially helpful in interpreting the junior viewpoint to your club. Some clubs offer annual awards to the top-winning Junior Handler who is a club member. This encourages juniors, provides recognition for juniors that may not always get the coveted first place but have a good overall record, encourages support of junior showmanship classes, and may encourage more youths to get involved. Other clubs offer their top junior handler financial assistance to attend the finals at Westminster Kennel Club. If your club doesn't provide such recognition, your influence can make a difference.

PROMOTE AWARDS

Nothing provides a higher incentive for achievement than offering an award for an outstanding performance. Trophies, rosettes, certificates, and cash all attract high achievers to competitions. If you have become active in a local kennel club, encourage the show committee to offer some exciting awards to the winning Junior Handlers at club sponsored shows and matches. You could even volunteer to help find individuals to sponsor the trophies.

Another possibility is to ask your club to offer a trophy to the Junior member of the club who best demonstrates the qualities of good sportsmanship. Breed clubs might consider offering yearly trophies to the Junior Handler with the highest number of wins showing their breed of dog. The trophy could be awarded on a point-scale basis. A first-place from the Open classes is worth ten points. Second-place is worth five points, third-place is worth three points, and fourth is worth one point.

START A JUNIOR SHOWMANSHIP CLUB

If there are enough interested juniors in your area, you could start your own club. To recruit members, look through show catalogs for junior handlers to contact. You can also talk to juniors at shows and ask area clubs if they have any junior members or sons and daughters of members who might be interested in joining your club. If you think you have a small but enthusiastic group you can count on, set a date, time, and place for your first meeting.

Set up some initial guidelines under which your club will operate, even if you plan to be informal. Then start collecting ideas for a more formal constitution. Many Junior Showmanship clubs already in existence will be willing to share their experiences in writing a constitution. Perhaps you could read the constitution

of a local kennel club to get ideas. Basically, your constitution should cover membership eligibility, dues (if any), guidelines for officers, and the purpose for which the club was organized.

Some possible goals for your club include working to reduce high entry fees for Junior Showmanship classes at area shows, educating juniors about possible careers and hobbies associated with purebred dogs, fostering good sportsmanship, and training juniors in the art of handling. Good ways to exchange ideas, improve skills, and make friends are to hold practice handling sessions. If you open these sessions to the public, you may recruit new members and educate others about Junior Showmanship.

Some possible club activities include:
- inviting guest speakers from various fields within the dog world;
- showing some of the many American Kennel Club (AKC) films available (maybe for a small fee);
- holding steward classes to help educate members in ring procedures;
- organizing general dog-care classes or individual programs on dog health care, dog anatomy, etc.;
- fund-raising for the club through bake sales, etc.;
- developing community awareness programs to promote public interest in the sport; and
- meeting regularly to discuss news and happenings in the Junior Showmanship world.

These are just a few ideas on forming your own club. Your contacts with adults in the sport will give you additional ideas. The one necessary ingredient is a group of members who will work together for the benefit of the club. Why not give it a try?

JOIN JUNIOR DOG FANCIERS OF AMERICA
Brandi Smith, a former junior handler from Birmingham, Alabama, formed a national organization for juniors in 1991. One of the club's goals is to educate and entice kennel clubs and individual adult fanciers to become more involved with juniors. Services to members include a certification program for junior showmanship instructors and help for novices looking for qualified trainers. You can write to the Junior Dog Fanciers of America at 2809 Arrowhead Circle, Birmingham, AL 35215, or call (205) 854-2370.

When You Are To Old To Compete In Junior Classes

BECOME A JUNIOR SHOWMANSHIP JUDGE
You're not over the hill at age 18! Thanks to the efforts of the Junior Handlers Association (which is no longer in existence), and the support of many other individuals and organizations, the AKC has agreed to accept judging applications from former Junior Handlers who have reached their eighteenth birthday and can no longer compete in classes. In the summer of 1974, the AKC

released news of a program that would allow former Junior Handlers to become licensed judges for Junior Showmanship classes at AKC licensed shows.

Any former Junior Handler over the age of 17 is eligible to send a judging application form to the AKC for consideration. The AKC makes final approvals by following nearly the same procedures as it does for a breed or an obedience judge's application.

Many young adults, mostly under the age of 21, have been asked to judge Junior Showmanship classes at all-breed and specialty shows. They draw excellent entries, and entrants are pleased to be judged by former junior handlers. Additionally, kennel clubs are favorably impressed with the abilities of these young judges to handle their assignments.

If you are sincerely interested in becoming a licensed Junior Showmanship judge, write to the AKC for a judging application form. Fill out the entire form carefully before you send it back.

You will receive notification from the AKC whether your application was approved or not. Upon approval, the AKC grants you what is called *provisional status*. This means you must judge at least five shows as a Provisional Judge with a representative from the AKC evaluating your performance.

Once you have completed five shows as a Provisional Judge, you must notify the AKC that you have completed these assignments. The AKC will again review your application along with the remarks written up by the AKC representative who viewed you in the ring. The AKC judge's committee will notify you of their decision. Hopefully it will be in your favor, and you will be on your way as a Junior Showmanship judge! Always remember how you felt when you were showing and strive to be an encouragement to young handlers. A harsh, insensitive judge can discourage a youth from ever handling again. A sensitive, helpful judge can have a great deal of positive influence.

If the AKC's decision to grant you judging status is not favorable, don't give up. You might need a little more experience, which you can pick up at fun matches. Check with the AKC to see if you can reapply later.

Don't be discouraged; your support is always needed in other areas. Volunteer to steward at the Junior Showmanship rings, or assist a local trainer in giving handling lessons to juniors or adults. You might even start your own handling class.

PROFESSIONAL HANDLING

Many junior handlers go on to become paid professional handlers who make their living by showing dogs for other owners. Good junior handlers are often in demand for summer or after school work for breeder exhibitors, professional handlers, or groomers. Any of these jobs will give you further exposure to the world of dogs. You will gain valuable skills that will help you if you do decide to make handling a career.

CONTINUE YOUR EDUCATION

Your experience handling dogs and your exposure to other aspects of dogs can be valuable in preparing you for many dog-related careers or hobbies. Perhaps you want to be a veterinarian, or work as a vet tech. The knowledge of dog behavior, health, and preventive care you gained during your years as a junior handler will give you an edge over someone without practical experience.

Perhaps you like to write and your secret desire is to become a newspaper columnist or magazine editor writing about dogs. You may aspire to a career in drawing, painting, or photographing dogs. The knowledge you have gained about various breeds of dogs, their characteristics and problems, and the eye you have developed for stacking and presenting them in the show ring could be invaluable in these careers.

The Dog Writer's Association of America sponsors an annual Dog Writer's Educational Trust Award to young adults who wish to pursue their education in relation to dogs. Applicants must submit an essay and application. The DWAA Board of Trustees assesses the need, scholastic ability, and potential of each candidate and awards a cash scholarship to further the education of the winning applicant.

Judith Strom

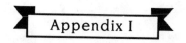

THE 4-H DOG PROGRAM

The focus of 4-H animal programs is on teaching boys and girls to raise and understand animals. Since many youths do not live on a farm and are unable to keep larger animals such as horses and cows, the 4-H Dog Program is one of several that provides an opportunity for youths to get involved with smaller animals.

There is no membership fee for 4-H. To get involved with the 4-H Dog Program, you must have either a pure or mixed breed dog; you must be between the ages of 9 and 19. As with all the 4-H animal programs, the Dog Program is an excellent tool for character development. It encourages young adults to acquire patience and persistence and to achieve their goals. The 4-H Dog Program concentrates more on the skills of training and presenting dogs than on the physical makeup of the dog, as is emphasized in conformation classes at dog shows.

You will need to find a group in your area. You can do this by contacting the County Government Office in your immediate area and asking for the Cooperative Extension Office. If you don't have a County Government Office in your area, contact a land grant college or university in your state. They'll be able to put you in contact with someone in your area who can assist you in your search. To locate land grant colleges and universities in your state, visit the reference section of your local library. If there is no group in your area, organize your own group. You'll need other interested young adults and a volunteer leader.

You will gain significant experience in the 4-H Dog Program. The competition is equal to that in the Junior Showmanship ring; but you can show a mixed breed of dog. Plus, you'll meet many young people who share your similar interest in and love for dogs and you will learn a great deal about dogs and their care.

Many boys and girls who started out with 4-H Dog Program have later developed careers in dog-related fields. The career opportunities are endless—from becoming a veterinarian to working as a professional dog handler.

History of 4-H

The concept of 4-H originated in the early 1900s from public school corn clubs for boys and canning clubs for girls. In 1914,

Congress passed the Smith-Lever Act, creating the Cooperative Extension Services, which in turn created the 4-H Youth Education Program. Today, it is the largest youth organization in the world, serving over 3,000 counties in the United States alone.

The Program's original goal was to serve youths through fostering their growing interests in agriculture and home economics. Today, however, 4-H has broadened its service programs to keep pace with and reflect prevalent social changes.

The initial growth period stemmed from the increased demand on the federal government to produce more food during World War I. So, the government increased its funding to the Cooperative Extension Services, which expanded the 4-H Program, and consequently increased food production.

The growth and popularity of the 4-H Program continued to thrive through the 1920s, when the National Committee on Boy's and Girl's Club Work was formed to help encourage the private sector to support 4-H and all its endeavors. After World War II, 4-H expanded into other countries. In 1959, the National 4-H Center opened in Chevy Chase, Maryland, serving as a training facility. In 1976, the National 4-H Council was created.

The continued growth of the 4-H Program is dependent upon its thousands of volunteer leaders who freely donate their time and knowledge. Without this support, 4-H would not have developed into the successful program it is today. Other support comes from parents; USDA-sponsored land grant colleges and universities; from Congress; and from major corporations. Ralston Purina regularly supports the National 4-H Dog Care and Training Development Committee through its financial and technical assistance.

The 4-H symbol is the four-leaf clover, with the "H" representing the program's fourfold aim of improving the Head, Heart, Hands, and Health of youth.

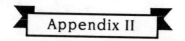

Appendix II

HOW TO REGISTER YOUR PUPPY

If you have just purchased a new puppy, it is important that you take care of all the paperwork right away. You will receive either a blue litter registration slip or a white individual dog registration paper on which the breeder or previous owner has assigned ownership to you. If the dog has already been registered by name, all you have to do is sign the back of the form and send it to the AKC with the appropriate transfer fee.

If you received a blue slip of paper, you must name your dog and send the application to the AKC to obtain the dog's registration papers. At the top front of the form you will see a space for the name you select for your dog. The name (words and spaces) must fit into the number of blocks provided on the form. As you can see, it is limited in length to 26 spaces.

If the breeder of your puppy has asked you to use his or her kennel's name in your dog's name, it is a nice courtesy to do so. Many breeders work very hard to establish their own bloodline and build a reputation for winning dogs. The addition of a kennel name in front or at the end of a name identifies your puppy as being from that particular bloodline. Unless the kennel is very famous and the name has been registered with the AKC, you do not need the breeder's signature for permission to use the kennel name.

Below this you will see listed the dog's breed, date of birth, litter number, and the name of the sire, the dam, and the dog's breeder. The litter number is the same for every puppy from that same litter, and is not the same thing as a dog's registration number. It is a good idea to make an extra copy of this side of the form because you must have this information in order to enter your dog in an AKC dog show.

On the back of the form you will find a space that you must fill in with your name and address. Above that the breeder will have filled out the transfer information and the previous owner or owners must have signed the form here.

If you are going to co-own your dog with another family member or with the breeder, both names and addresses must be entered and you must BOTH sign the form. The co-owner whose name and address appear first is the one who will receive the registration form and any other communication from the AKC.

You must mail the form with the amount listed to the American Kennel Club at the address on the form. This must be done before the puppy is one year of age, so it is important to do it right away. A few weeks later you will receive a white form with the name of your puppy and with you listed as owner on it. This is a very important document. Keep it in a safe place, and once again make a copy so that you have the information easily available when the time comes to make out your show entry forms. If for any reason you later sell or give the dog to someone else, you will need the registration slip in order to transfer the dog to its new owner.

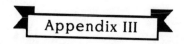

Appendix III

THE PUPPY PLACEMENT PROGRAM

In the past, Mr. Paul Nigro, who was the Junior Showmanship columnist for *Dog World* magazine, and a fervent supporter of junior events, set up a program which provided the opportunity to acquire a show quality purebred dog for junior handlers who couldn't afford a puppy. Through Mr. Nigro, the junior handler would be introduced to a purebred dog breeder. If the youth agreed to abide by the requirements of the breeder, an agreement would be drawn up which allowed him or her to co-own or own and show the dog.

This program is now inactive, but many national breed clubs have continued where the Puppy Placement Program left off. These clubs have developed Junior Showmanship committees which successfully match juniors in search of a dog of their particular breed with a breeder willing to work with them.

Remember, anything is possible if you are really dedicated. If you are determined to get into junior handling but cannot afford a dog, contact the American Kennel Club for the address of the national breed club secretary for the breed or breeds in which you are interested. Then write and ask if they have this type of program. Of course, you can also locate breeders in your own area and perhaps exchange kennel help or other after school work for a puppy.

Best Jr. Handler– A Junior Showmanship competition. The handler who placed first in each of the regular classes at a show are automatically eligible to compete.

Bitch– A female dog.

Brace– Two dogs being shown together.

Breed– The official name of a pure strain of dogs; or (verb) to arrange a mating of male and female dogs.

Breeder– The person listed as breeder on a dog's registration form; the person(s) who planned the mating that produced this individual dog.

Color– On an entry form, refers to the coat color of the dog. Used in breeds where judging is divided according to color.

Conformation– Form and structure; arrangement of parts in conformance to the demands of the breed standard. Also used as a generic reference to dog show breed classes.

Dam– The female parent.

Dog– A male dog; often used to designate either a male or female dog.

Futurity– A competition for young dogs nominated at or before birth.

Handler– A person handling a dog in the show ring or field trial.

Height– Vertical measurement from the withers to the ground; often referred to as *Shoulder Height*.

ILP Number– Independent Listing Number assigned to a dog that is certified as purebred but whose sire and/or dam are not registered with the AKC.

Litter– A group of puppies born on the same day to the same parents, i.e., full brothers and sisters with the same birth date.

Litter Number– The number assigned by the parent club to all the puppies in one litter.

Monorchid– A male dog with only one testicle visible.

Novice Junior– Showmanship class for boys or girls at least 10 years old and under 14 years old on the day of the show who have not won 3 first place awards in a Novice class in a licensed or member show.

Novice Senior– For boys and girls at least 14 years old and under 18 years old who have not won 3 first place awards in a Novice Senior class at a licensed or member show.

Open Junior– For boys and girls at least 10 years old and under 18 years old who have won 3 or more first place awards in a Novice Class at a licensed or member show.

Open Senior– For boys and girls at least 14 years old and under 18 years old who have won 3 or more first place awards in a Novice Class at a licensed or member show.

Professional Handler– A person who handles dogs in the show ring for other people, usually for pay. Also called an Agent.

Registration Number– The individual number assigned to each dog by the AKC or other official registry for that breed.

Sire– The male parent.

Steward– The person who assists the judge in the show ring.

Variety– The subdivision of a breed into various sizes or types, such as Standard, Miniature, or Toy, Smooth or Rough Coated, etc.

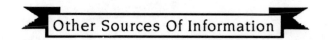
Other Sources Of Information

RULES APPLYING TO JUNIOR SHOWMANSHIP

It is important that you acquire a current copy of the booklet "Junior Showmanship Regulations, Judging Guidelines, and Guidelines for Juniors" from the AKC and study it carefully.

Phone (212) 696-8281 or write to:

American Kennel Club
Events Records Department
51 Madison Avenue
New York, New York 10010

AKC Registration Information

American Kennel Club
5580 Centerview Drive
Raleigh, NC 27606
(919) 233-9767

ORGANIZATIONS

Canadian Kennel Club
89 Skyway Avenue
Etobicoke, Ontario, Canada M9W 6R4

Junior Dog Fanciers Club of America (JDFCA)
2809 Arrowhead Circle
Birmingham, AL 35215
(205) 854-2370

National 4-H Dog Project Director
National 4-H Council
7100 Connecticut Ave.
Chevy Chase, MD 20815

States Kennel Club
P. O. Box 389
Hattiesburg, MS 39403-0389

United Kennel Club
100 East Kilgore Road
Kalamazoo, MI 49001

World Series of Junior Showmanship
Newport Dog Shows
128 N. Fair Oaks Blvd.
Pasadena, CA 91103
(818) 796-3869

PUBLICATIONS

Books

All About Dog Shows
Sam Kohl
Aaronco
ISBN 0-876666-72-1

Canine Terminology
Harold R. Spira
Howell Book House
ISBN 0-06-312047-X

Dog Showing: An Owner's Guide
Connie Vanacore
Howell Book House
ISBN 0-87605-524-2

Junior Handling: The Complete Guide on How to Show Your Dog
Cosme
Ringpr Books, U.K.
Seven Hills Book Distributors
ISBN 0-948955-51-1

Junior Showmanship Handbook
Brown/Maso
Howell Book House
ISBN 0-87605-655-9

The Winning Edge: Show Ring Secrets
George Alston with Connie Vanacore
Howell Book House
ISBN 0-87605-834-9

Your Purebred Puppy; A Buyer's Guide
Michele Lowell
Henry Holt & Company
ISBN 0-8050-1411-X

Dog Book Catalogs

Direct Book Service
P. O. Box 3073
Wenatchee, WA 98807

4-M Enterprises, Inc.
1280 Pacific Street
Union City, CA 94587

Magazines

Bloodlines (Official UKC publication)
100 E. Kilgore Rd.
Kalamazoo, MI 49001

Dogs in Canada (Official CKC publication)
43 Railside Road
Don Mills, Ontario, Canada M3A 3L9

Dog Fancy
Business Office & Advertising:
P.O. Box 57900
Los Angeles, CA 90057-0900
Subscriptions:
P.O. Box 53264
Boulder, CO 80322-3264

Dog World
29 North Wacker Drive
Chicago, IL 60606

Purebred Dogs, The AKC Gazette
51 Madison Avenue
New York, NY 10010

Index

Other Titles from Alpine Publications

How to Raise A Puppy You Can Live With
Clarice Rutherford and David H. Neil, M.R.C.V.S.
A guide to raising, training, and socializing a puppy from birth to one year of age.
2nd Edition, 1991.
ISBN 0-931866-57-X

Positively Obedient: Good Manners for the Family Dog
Barbara Handler
Easy, positive methods for training good behavior and basic commands like "sit," "stay," and "heel," plus information on care, grooming and responsible dog ownership.
ISBN 0-931866-28-6

The New Secrets of Show Dog Handling
Mario Migliorini
A beginning guide to the art of handling a dog in the show ring, insights into judging, tips on handling various breeds, and more.
ISBN 0-931866-

Successful Obedience Handling
Barbara Handler
How to polish your own and your dog's obedience performance to achieve better scores in obedience competition—Novice through Open classes.
ISBN 0-931866-51-0

201 Ways to Enjoy Your Dog
Ellie Milon
Learn about hundreds of organized competitions and activities you can do with your dog. Brief descriptions, names and addresses of organizations, and more.
ISBN 0-931866-33-2

Available from your local book or pet supply dealer, or call 1-800-777-7257 for ordering information and prices.